Jaguar F-Type

THE COMPLETE STORY

ANDREW NOAKES

THE CROWOOD PRESS

First published in 2020 by
The Crowood Press Ltd
Ramsbury, Marlborough
Wiltshire SN8 2HR

enquiries@crowood.com

www.crowood.com

This impreesion 2023

British Library Cataloguing-in-Publication Data
A catalogue record for this book is available from the British Library.

ISBN 978 1 78500 731 6

Acknowledgements
In telling the story of the F-types I have been able to call upon numerous excellent sources of information and images. The authors of contemporary press reports are too numerous to mention, but I thank them all for the insight and context they bring to the tale. Ian Callum generously gave me his time to talk about the Aston Martin DB7 and its genesis from the abortive Jaguar XJ41/42 F-type for a previous Crowood book. Richard Towns, Ed Superfon and Michael Gulett kindly provided images of the Owen Sedanca, Bertone Pirana and Raymond Loewy E-type respectively. Former Jaguar men Martin Broomer, Keith Helfet, César Pieri and Martin Joyce provided input on the XJ41/42, XK180, F-type/X600 and Project 7. Ex-Jaguar test driver Norman Dewis provided personal recollections of his work on earlier Jaguar sports cars, and journalist Ray Hutton filled in some gaps on the Pininfarina XJ Spider. Other vital input and assistance came from Steve Cropley and Max Adams at *Autocar*, James Taylor at *CAR*, car design lecturer Aamer Mahmud at Coventry University, Tony Merrygold at Jaguar Heritage, and Adam Price at Tom Lenthall Ltd. My thanks to each of them for the information, encouragement, corrections and suggestions they have provided.

Typeset and designed by D & N Publishing, Baydon, Wiltshire

Printed and bound in India by Parksons Graphics Pvt. Ltd.

CONTENTS

TIMELINE

1974   E-type production ends

1975   XJ-S unveiled

1978   Pininfarina XJ Spider unveiled at the Birmingham International Motor show

1980   XJ40 saloon project approved

1990   XJ41/42 project cancelled

1996   XK8 introduced

1998   XK180 concept

2000   F-type concept

2011   C-X16 concept

2012   F-type unveiled at the Paris motor show

2013   F-type Coupé and V8 R, Project 7 concept

2014   F-type AWD models

2015   Project 7 production car

2016   F-type SVR

2017   F-type facelift, 400 Sport and R-Dynamic models; F-type 4-cylinder

2019   Revised F-type announced

INTRODUCTION

How do you replace an icon? It's a question Jaguar struggled with for more than forty years, from the final days of the seminal E-type in the early 1970s right through to the second decade of the twenty-first century.

With the E-type, Jaguar had created a sports car with an enduring appeal thanks to its combination of dramatic looks, searing performance and extraordinary value. But producing a successor proved to be difficult. The XJ-S of 1975 was a very different kind of car, more aimed at providing comfort and refinement in long-distance fast cruising than at delivering the keen responses demanded by an enthusiastic driver. Though there were several proposals over the years for genuine Jaguar sports cars in the E-type mould, both from within Jaguar and from external designers, it took until 2012 for a genuine successor to finally appear.

This book traces the journey Jaguar took to the production F-type, along the way examining the iconic status of the E-type, and looking at the cars down the years that might have become the F-type but never quite made the grade.

Just as there are numerous candidates to be called the fifth Beatle, there's a surprisingly long list of cars and concepts that could, and in some cases perhaps should, have assumed the F-type mantle. Jaguar's own XJ-S and Pininfarina's XJ Spider concept are both on that list, alongside a number of abortive concept machines and the XK production cars. Then, of course, there is the F-type itself, in concept form and finally as a production reality.

It's a fascinating story, not just because of the variety of machinery involved and the twists and turns of the development processes, but also because the trials and tribulations, and the ultimate success of the F-type idea, dovetail with the wider story of Jaguar as a marque. Its struggles as part of the ill-fated British Leyland combine, followed by its independence and renewal and stability, first under Ford's ownership and later under Tata's, are mirrored in the early uncertainty over what an F-type should be, and the eventual realization of a worthy successor to the brand's most famous car.

CHAPTER ONE

FORERUNNERS: BEFORE THE F-TYPE

The road to the Jaguar F-type was full of twists and turns, and they started right at the beginning of the story. This was because the company that became Jaguar started out building something other than cars, and the man who was the driving force behind it originally had a passion not for motor cars, but for motorbikes.

William Lyons was born in Blackpool, on the north-west coast of England, in 1901. His father, also William, was an Irish

immigrant who ran a music shop. William junior was not much of a scholar, but was encouraged by his father to join Crossley Motors in Manchester at the age of sixteen as an engineering apprentice. Crossley built fine cars, and during World War I, its chassis formed the basis for military trucks and ambulances.

But Lyons was not happy at Crossley, and in 1919 he joined Brown and Mallalieu, a motor car dealer at the Metropole Garage in Josiah Street, Blackpool, as a junior salesman. He had an aptitude for the work, and it allowed him to indulge on the side in his passion for motorcycles. Lyons was already trading in two-wheelers, and by the time he was twenty he had owned examples of many different marques, including Sunbeam, Indian, Norton and Harley-Davidson.

It was good fortune, then, that in 1921 William Walmsley moved into King Edward Avenue, close to where Lyons lived, and began rebuilding army surplus motorcycles for civilian use. He also designed a sidecar with octagonal bodywork in polished aluminium, which he offered for sale at £28. In an era when a sidecar body was either a large wicker basket or something with an alarming resemblance to a tin bath, Walmsley's streamlined aluminium model was new and exciting. Lyons bought one, and spotted its potential straight away.

EARLY DEVELOPMENTS

Lyons and Walmsley were soon working together. Lyons envisaged production on a much grander scale than Walms-

William Lyons in the 1920s astride a Harley-Davidson 11-F motorcycle. The bike appears to be prepared for speed, with no headlamp or speedo, and lowered handlebars.
JAGUAR

ley's rate of one a week, and this necessitated moving into larger premises. With a £1,000 bank loan guaranteed by their respective fathers, Lyons and Walmsley set up at Bloomfield Road in Blackpool. Lyons was still twenty and too young to enter into a legal business agreement, but shortly after his twenty-first birthday he formed an official partnership with Walmsley and the Swallow Sidecar Company was born.

The Swallow Sidecar Company

Lyons had already demonstrated the aptitude for salesmanship and business acumen that were to be notable throughout his career, and now he showed another trait that would serve him well down the years – as a showman. When Swallow went to the Motorcycle Show in London in November 1922 to display its sidecars, Lyons and Walmsley rode bikes to London with the sidecars attached. But these were not just any bikes – they were Brough Superiors, the finest British motorcycles of the day.

Swallow's sidecars sold well, and the company expanded into larger premises in Cocker Street, Blackpool, to cope with demand. It was there that Swallow branched out to build special bodywork for cars, initially the popular Austin Seven.

At £175 the Austin Seven Swallow was a stylish and individual small car at a bargain price, and it was a huge success.

As the company continued to grow it became obvious that a location closer to the manufacturing centre of the British motor industry in the Midlands would be advantageous. Shortening the lines of communication with suppliers and the journeys between their factories and the Swallow works would cut costs and improve production flexibility. So in 1928 what was by then the Swallow Coachbuilding Company moved 130 miles south from Blackpool to the city of Coventry, already regarded as the centre of the British motor industry. They took up residence in a former munitions factory off Holbrook Lane in Foleshill, a couple of miles north of the city centre.

SS Cars

Swallow became a proper car maker thanks to the support of another Coventry-based automotive company: Standard. The Standard Motor Company supplied Lyons and Walmsley with engines, transmissions and chassis for the SS1, the first car that was a genuine Swallow product, rather than a bespoke body for a car made by someone else. The SS1

Swallow Model 4 Super Sports sidecar from 1928, fitted to a 1925 Brough Superior SS80. William Walmsley's sidecars were very modern for their time and sold well.
AUTHOR

An SS1 saloon at the 2014 Salon Privé event. The SS1 was the first complete car built by SS.

was announced at the London motor show in 1931 and had attractive, rakish lines – but it was not a performance car. Rather, Lyons had spotted a gap in the market for a car offering fine styling and value for money, and it proved to be another success for the fledgling firm. By now Walmsley was happy with what Swallow had achieved and had no real ambitions to do more, but Lyons wanted to go further. He created a new company, SS Cars, and bought out Walmsley's share to become sole managing director.

In 1935 SS introduced its first proper sports car, the two-seat SS90, but like previous SS models, it was still more about styling than performance. To address this William Heynes was brought in from Hillman to be chief engineer, and engine expert Harry Weslake was engaged to redesign the Standard engine. Weslake produced an overhead valve layout with a crossflow cylinder head, and in this form the engine developed 102bhp, a massive leap from the Standard's 70bhp. The revised engine went into a new saloon car called the SS Jaguar, and then into the sports car to produce the SS Jaguar 100. In 3½-litre form this car was capable of 100mph

(160km/h) – quite something for the 1930s. Finally Lyons had built a car with genuinely impressive performance to match the stunning styling that had always been an SS hallmark.

But the SS sports cars were not in production for long. With the onset of war in 1939 private car production was stopped, and SS turned its manufacturing facilities over to the production of aircraft components, including centre fuselage sections for the new Gloster Meteor, the first British jet fighter. But the war years were not entirely devoid of car-making activity – in fact two key decisions were taken by Lyons during this period which would have far-reaching effects for the company after the war.

The first came when John Black told Lyons in 1942 that Standard would be making a new range of engines after the war and would no longer supply SS with the existing units. Spotting the chance to become self-sufficient, Lyons immediately offered to buy all the tooling and equipment necessary to manufacture the existing engines. As soon as the deal was struck he had trucks and workmen at Standard's Canley factory ready to remove all the equipment and take

The SS100 established Lyons' reputation for stunning looks and high performance at a good price.

it to Foleshill before Black, a famously moody and capricious operator, could change his mind.

As it turned out Black did indeed think twice, realizing too late that he had seriously curtailed the range of engines that Standard could now build for itself. 'It wasn't long before Black proposed that we should revert to the previous arrangement, and return the plant to Standard,' said Lyons in a paper he presented to the Institute of the Motor Industry in 1969. 'He pressed me very hard, even to the extent of suggesting that we should form a separate company together.' When Black suggested Lyons return the engine tooling to Standard, Lyons is said to have replied: 'No thank you, John, I have got the ball now, and I would rather kick it myself.'

The XK Engine

But while Lyons took the opportunity to secure the supply of engines for the short term, he was also looking at the long-term future of his company. That meant a new, more powerful engine, one that started to take shape during the war years. SS staff were among many workers across Coventry who took turns to 'fire watch' at night, and Lyons saw to it that chief engineer Heynes and engine designers Walter Hassan and Claude Baily were on watch at the same time, so they could spend the time discussing the new engine. In-line and V engines with 4, 6, 8 and 12 cylinders were all considered during these long night-time vigils, but eventually Heynes and his team opted for an in-line 6-cylinder unit. The result was the XK engine, a 3442cc motor with double overhead camshafts, opposed valves and hemispherical combustion chambers, which made its debut in 1948.

A NEW MARQUE: JAGUAR CARS

By then another important decision had been made. During the war the Nazi political police, the Schutzstaffel, had given the initials 'SS' connotations that Lyons must have been keen to avoid. The SS was, he later commented, 'a sector of the community that was not highly regarded'. So in 1945 SS Cars adopted the name of its most famous models to become Jaguar Cars, and a new marque was born. The pre-war SS Jaguar 1½-litre, 2½-litre and 3½-litre saloons were relaunched after the war carrying just the Jaguar name – but behind-the-scenes work was under way on the new MkV Jaguar saloon to take the rebranded company into the 1950s.

Just before the outbreak of war a new independent front suspension had been developed to replace the beam axle and leaf springs of the Standard-based cars. Coil springs and oil/air struts were investigated, but eventually Heynes and Walter Hassan settled on a double wishbone layout with the bottom wishbone splined to a longitudinal torsion bar spring that was anchored at the bottom of the front bulkhead, the strongest part of the structure. When development resumed in earnest after the war, a new chassis was drawn up with deep box-section side members, giving great strength, with a cross-shaped brace to ensure a high degree of torsional stiffness.

The XK120

By early 1948, work on the chassis was well advanced – but the XK engine was not yet ready for volume production, and that turned out to be a blessing in disguise for Jaguar. Lyons realized that the new engine could be used in a low-volume sports car, which could trial the motor among enthusiastic buyers who would tolerate any problems more readily than would Jaguar's saloon customers. The new sports car would

also generate plenty of interest – but there was little time to get it ready if it was to be on show at the first post-war London motor show at Earls Court in October 1948.

To form the basis of the sports car the MkV chassis was shortened and narrowed, which made it naturally stiffer. That meant the substantial cruciform bracing of the saloon chassis could be replaced by a simple box-section cross-member. Suspension, brakes and steering were all carried over from the saloon. The body that covered the mechanicals was, as ever, designed under Lyons' personal control, and introduced a new and much more modern style to Jaguar's cars, with the wings integrated into the body for the first time. Reputedly from first sketch to finished metal took just two weeks.

The resulting car, the XK120, was the star of the London motor show. To a country starved of much in the way of good news, and downtrodden from years of scrimping, saving and rationing, it was an extraordinary statement of the capability of British industry and the future of the country. Not only did this new sports car look impossibly fast and exotic, it also promised a top speed of 120mph (193km/h) and was offered at the astonishingly low price of £998 before tax.

Jaguar had planned a short production run using hand-built aluminium alloy bodies, but received so many orders during the show that genuine series production was a necessity, and a deal was quickly done with Pressed Steel to supply steel panels. The first XK120s did have alloy bodies, as they were built while the tooling for the steel body was still being made. Early road tests were resoundingly positive, praising the performance and the exceptional ride quality, though there was criticism for the cramped cabin, and the combination of all-enveloping bodywork and steel disc wheels reduced air flow to the drum brakes, causing them to fade.

The XK120 of 1948 introduced the twin-cam engine that would power Jaguars for the next half-century.
JAGUAR

RACING JAGUARS – C-TYPE, D-TYPE AND XJ13

The XK120C (C for competition) or C-type was built specifically for racing. The engine was a tuned version of the existing XK unit, but the chassis was all new, a multi-tube frame that was lighter than the XK120's ladder chassis, though more expensive to make. Jaguar entered three cars for the 1951 Le Mans 24-hour race, and while two retired, the third car, driven by Peter Walker and Peter Whitehead, won the race.

The XK120C or 'C-type' was the first Jaguar purpose-built for racing.
JAGUAR

Birth of the D-type: Tony Rolt in XKD401, the first car, at Le Mans testing in 1954.
JAGUAR

continued overleaf

RACING JAGUARS – C-TYPE, D-TYPE AND XJ13 *continued*

ABOVE: **The D-type, designed to win at Le Mans, introduced aircraft construction principles.**

XJ13, here with Jaguar test driver Norman Dewis, was a spectacular V12-engined racer, but it arrived too late to be competitive.
JAGUAR

For 1952 Jaguar revised the C-types with low-drag bodywork and revised cooling, but all three cars retired with engine failures. The C-types were back to form in 1953, winning the race again and at record speed, in part due to the fitment of disc brakes for the first time. But the win came in curious circumstances: drivers Duncan Hamilton and Tony Rolt were disqualified after their car carried the wrong number during a practice session. Fortunately Jaguar team manager 'Lofty' England eventually persuaded the organizers to relent, but legend has it that the drivers had already repaired to a local bar to drown their sorrows. Hamilton started the race having been judged the soberer of the pair, and hot coffee was provided at pit stops…

For 1954 Jaguar developed the D-type, again using a development of the XK engine but in a completely different structure based on aircraft principles. The main part was a stressed-skin tub, to which a tubular subframe was bolted to carry the engine and front suspension. The body shape created by aerodynamicist Malcolm Sayer aimed to minimize drag on the long Mulsanne straight at Le Mans, where they proved significantly quicker than the rival Ferraris in 1954. But engine problems denied Jaguar another victory until 1955, when Mike Hawthorn and Ivor Bueb won after the Mercedes-Benz team withdrew following the accident that killed Pierre Levegh and more than eighty spectators.

The D-type won Le Mans twice more, in 1956 and 1957, in the hands of the Scottish privateer team Écurie Écosse. The D-type did the job it was intended to do – win at Le Mans – but it was never very successful on other circuits, as its handling was inferior to the Ferraris and Aston Martins.

'We'd drive the cars to Le Mans, win the race and drive them back,' recalled test driver Norman Dewis years later. 'After Le Mans at four o'clock on Sunday when we won, Sir William would just walk over and say, "Well done Dewis". That's all you got.'

Jaguar then took a break from racing as a factory team, but it did build a small number of lightweight E-type racing cars in the mid-1960s, before developing the XJ13 in 1965. This mid-engined, V12-powered car was first mooted in 1960, but by the time it was ready in 1966 Ford had already stolen a march with the mid-engined GT40, and the XJ13 was mothballed. It was nearly destroyed in an accident during a demonstration run at MIRA in 1971, but was rebuilt and survives.

In May 1949 an XK120 appeared at the Jabbeke-Aeltre highway to prove it could really achieve 120mph (193km/h). Test driver Ron 'Soapy' Sutton recorded 126.448mph (203.5km/h) with the roof up, then with no roof or windscreen he achieved 132.596mph (213.4km/h). In 1950 Leslie Johnson and Stirling Moss averaged 107mph (172km/h) over twenty-four hours at Montlhéry in France, and Johnson returned the following year to cram 131 miles (211km) into an hour. In 1951 Jaguar introduced a two-seat fixed-head coupé XK120 and a Special Equipment model with stiffer suspension, higher-lift camshafts and a straight-through exhaust to generate a claimed 181bhp. Wire wheels also became an option, reducing brake fade by improving air flow.

Though too heavy for racing, the XK120 was ideally suited to rallies, where strength and reliability mattered more. Ian Appleyard's car, with the registration number NUB120, won the first ever Alpine Rally Gold Cup for three consecutive penalty-free runs, a feat only ever equalled by two other drivers. Appleyard's co-driver was his wife Patricia (née Lyons), daughter of Jaguar's founder. NUB120 is now one of the many iconic cars in the Jaguar Heritage Trust fleet based at the British Motor Museum in Gaydon.

In 1952 an XK120 fixed-head ran non-stop for seven days and nights at Montlhéry, covering almost 17,000 miles (27,000km) at an average of just over 100mph (160km/h). At Jabbeke in 1953 Norman Dewis recorded 142mph (229km/h) over a flying kilometre in a Special Equipment XK120 fitted with an aero screen, and later that year in a tuned XK120 fitted with a Perspex bubble canopy he recorded over 172mph (277km/h). 'That was a cracker,' Dewis told me in 2017. 'I was under a Perspex bubble, but the only thing was, they screwed the bubble down when I was in the car, and there was no bloody way I could have got out if I got into trouble.'

The XK140

In 1953 a drop-head coupé with an easy-to-erect, fully lined folding roof was added to the range, and then for 1954 the XK120 was replaced by the XK140, which introduced heavy, MkVII-style bumpers with substantial over-riders to satisfy the North American market, upgraded headlamps, and a mildly reworked front end. The engine and front bulkhead were pushed forward, and batteries relocated from behind the seats into the engine bay, to improve cabin space. The

NUB120 is probably the most famous XK120 of all. In this car Ian Appleyard won the first Alpine Rally gold cup for unpenalized runs in three consecutive years.

JAGUAR

XK140 was a refined version of the XK120 with better brakes, steering and suspension, and more interior space.

JAGUAR

dashboard was also raised slightly to make entry and exit easier. The engine now had a little more power, and there was the option of Laycock de Normanville overdrive – bringing more relaxed cruising and underlining the gradual shift in the XK's character from an out-and-out sports car to a fast grand touring machine. The XK120's recirculating ball steering was replaced by a rack-and-pinion system adapted from the C-type competition car.

The XK150

The XK140 sold even faster than the XK120 had done, finding nearly 9,000 buyers in little more than two years. In 1957 it was replaced by the XK150, which updated styling that was now looking a little old-fashioned, and added disc brakes, developed for the racing Jaguars, to finally cure the brake fade problems. The standard engine now developed

The XK150 replaced the XK140 in 1957, offering more power and better passenger accommodation than ever.
JAGUAR

Norman Dewis takes to the MIRA banking in a pre-production E-type around 1960. Production cars were not quite capable of the 150mph (240km/h) that Jaguar liked to claim.
JAGUAR

190bhp, and there was a Special Equipment version with larger exhaust valves offering 210bhp, and later an XK150S with 'straight port' head and triple carburettors. Ultimately the XK150 was available with a 265bhp 3.8-litre engine. Virtually the same engine went into the XK150's replacement in 1961, but this was more than just another iteration on the theme of the XK120. Instead, Jaguar introduced a new generation of sports car based very much on its successful D-type racing machine.

THE JAGUAR E-TYPE

The result was the E-type, and it caused an even bigger sensation on its launch at the Geneva motor show in March 1961 than the XK120 had at Earls Court thirteen years earlier. Like its forebear, it had remarkable styling – a devel-

opment of the low-drag D-type shape – and extraordinary performance. Jaguar claimed this new machine could top 150mph (241km/h), which meant it was the fastest road-going production car in the world. Only Jaguar could build such a rapid machine with such exciting lines, and yet put it on sale with a price of just £2,000 – not cheap, but still half the price of a Ferrari.

It was based on a stressed-skin tub similar to the D-type's, and was fitted with a triple-carb XK engine like the last of the XK150s, but the E-type incorporated new technology in the shape of independent rear suspension. Effectively this was a double-wishbone design with a fixed-length driveshaft acting as the top link. The rear disc brakes were mounted inboard, minimizing unsprung weight to improve ride and handling (though at the expense of more difficult maintenance). The layout was shared with the 420G and S-type saloons, and adopted on new Jaguars for many years to

---

Jaguar E-Type (1961) Specifications

Chassis and body		Suspension and steering	
Type	Steel monocoque chassis/body with front subframe; open two-seater, fixed-head two-seater, or fixed-head two-plus-two	Front	Double wishbones, torsion bars, telescopic dampers and anti-roll bar
		Rear	Lower wishbones, fixed-length drive shafts, twin coil springs with concentric dampers
Engine		Steering	Rack and pinion
Location	Front engine, longitudinal	Brakes	Front: solid discs
Block material	Iron		Rear: solid discs, inboard
Head material	Aluminium alloy		Servo assisted
Cylinders	6, in line		
Cooling	Water	Dimensions	
Lubrication	Wet sump	Length	4,445mm (175in)
Bore × stroke	87 × 106mm	Width	1,651mm (65in)
Capacity	3781cc	Height	1,219mm (48in)
Main bearings	Seven	Wheelbase	2,438mm (96in)
Valves/operation	2 valves per cylinder, twin chain-driven overhead camshafts	Unladen weight	1,270kg (2,800lb)
Compression ratio	9:1	Performance	
Fuel system	3 × SU HD8 carburettors	Top speed	241km/h (152mph)
Maximum power	265bhp gross at 5,500rpm	Acceleration	0–60mph: 7.2sec
Maximum torque	260lb/ft (353Nm) at 4,000rpm		
Transmission	Rear-wheel drive; Moss four-speed manual gearbox		

William Lyons faces the press with the new E-type in Geneva in March 1961.
JAGUAR

come. It gave an excellent ride and traction, and made most of the E-type's rivals look very old-fashioned.

The E-type was available in two forms: as an open-top roadster, and a sleek fastback coupé. Both were beautiful, with gently curving organic forms and a startling lack of ornamentation. Even the narrow front and rear tracks seemed to work for the E-type, making the body appear to float off the ground, when for many other cars they would have just looked weak. Enzo Ferrari, who had already been responsible for a few good-looking cars, said the Jaguar was the most beautiful car in the world. In truth, neither open nor closed E-types could quite hit the promised 150mph (241km/h) in production form, and the cars that motoring journalists drove were carefully prepared to ensure that they could actually reach the magic figure. But as well as praise for the E-type's prodigious speed – whatever its true maximum was – there were also brickbats for the restricted leg room and the slow, ponderous change of the Moss gearbox.

The E-type quickly became the car to be seen in. The first private owner of an E-type was French actor Jacques Charrier, husband of Brigitte Bardot, and many other entertainers had E-types, including George Harrison of The Beatles, Mick Jagger and Keith Richards of the Rolling Stones, Frank Sinatra, Roy Orbison, Diana Ross, Tommy Steele, radio DJ

77RW was one of the E-types displayed in Geneva in 1961, and was later road-tested by motoring journalists.
JAGUAR

Tony Blackburn, writer/director Bryan Forbes, and actors Charlton Heston, Tony Curtis and Rex Harrison.

Peter Sellers gave then-girlfriend Britt Eckland a red E-type roadster in 1967, and twice a week the closing credits of the BBC television talk show *Dee Time* showed host Simon Dee driving away from the studio in a white E-type. Footballer George Best, racing drivers Mike Hailwood and Bruce McLaren, and land speed record-holder Donald Campbell all had E-types too – among many other famous faces. The E-type became inextricably associated with the glamour and freedom of the 1960s, as much an icon of the decade as Twiggy, Apollo, or Andy Warhol's soup tins.

E-TYPE DEVELOPMENTS

In 1963 Jaguar built a dozen lightweight E-types for racing. The body panels were aluminium alloy rather than steel, and all the cars were roadsters with alloy hard tops. The suspension was stiffer, and there were Dunlop alloy wheels like those used on the D-type. The engine had an alloy block instead of the iron block of production XK engines, and had dry-sump lubrication. Using three Weber side-draught carburettors, or Lucas mechanical fuel injection, there was around 300bhp available, delivered through a close-ratio four-speed gearbox, or later a ZF five-speed. The lightweights proved to be competitive with Ferrari's 250GTOs, but they arrived just as GT racing was following the trend set by single-seater racing to mid-engined cars, and soon the E-types were outclassed in anything other than minor club events.

The road-going E-types were modified with a new floor to improve cabin space, and in 1964 the E-type adopted a 4.2-litre engine for more torque, together with a new Jaguar gearbox that offered a smoother change.

In 1966 Jaguar was taken over by the British Motor Corporation. BMC had already bought Pressed Steel, which supplied body panels to Jaguar, so the merger was really the only way Jaguar could guarantee supplies of vital components. Two years later, at the behest of the Labour government, the group merged with Leyland to form the British Leyland Motor Corporation.

By then Jaguar had added a 2+2 coupé to the range, with a longer wheelbase and higher roofline to provide space for two rear passengers, and had given the whole E-type range an update. There were open, rather than cowled, headlamps, rocker switches in place of toggle switches, new seats and

twin cooling fans – most of the changes being driven by regulations and customer demands in the US market. These 'Series 1½' cars were quickly supplanted by the Series 2, which introduced a larger front air intake to allow for the installation of air conditioning, plus larger and repositioned indicators. US-market cars were also detuned to meet stringent emissions regulations, using twin Stromberg carburettors instead of triple Sus: this resulted in a power loss of around 20bhp.

A New Engine: The V12

Jaguar's solution for the dwindling power output of the E-type – in the face of US muscle cars with ever greater power – was to introduce a new engine. Since the 1950s Jaguar had been considering a V12, and a 5.0-litre V12 race engine with double overhead cams per bank was built for the XJ13 in the 1960s. So now the V12 layout was back on the agenda as the optimum format for a large-capacity road-car engine that could deliver the power needed to restore the performance of the E-type to acceptable levels, and go on to power Jaguar saloons for years to come.

The new V12 was very different to the race engine. It adopted flat-faced cylinder heads with Heron combustion chambers sunk into the piston crowns, and on each bank of cylinders the valves were operated by a single chain-driven overhead camshaft. With a capacity of 5.3 litres in production form the engine delivered 295bhp in European specification, and at least 240bhp for the USA, depending on specification. Norman Dewis recalled its first road trials:

> The V12 was an incredible engine. Wally Hassan had done all the work on a test bed and got the engine ready. The idea was that we were going to introduce it in the E-type, but unfortunately they hadn't got the E-type chassis modified ready to take the V12 so it stood in the shop for two weeks. In those days we didn't like a job hanging about, and one evening I was in the workshop and there was a MkX with the engine out, and I thought 'I wonder if the V12 would go in there'. I got my tape measure out of the office and worked out that if we moved the engine mountings three inches forward we could get the V12 in. The following morning I talked to Phil Weaver,

OPPOSITE: **Williams Lyons at his home, Wappenbury Hall, probably in late 1966, with a 'Series 1½' E-type.**
JAGUAR

FORERUNNERS: BEFORE THE F-TYPE

the superintendent – that was eight o'clock in the morning – and by five in the afternoon the V12 was in the MkX.

I used to take it home, and one Sunday morning I went to see some friends at Luton, down the M1. I got behind this Mk2 saloon and just sat behind him. He must have seen me in the mirror and pushed on a bit, and we got up to 100, 110, 120, then I pulled out, got alongside and passed him. On the Monday morning I went in and security rang me and said 'Norman, a guy's been on the phone, said a MkX passed him when he was doing 125mph. Have you got a special MkX?' I said, ring him back and say if he finds out who it was, could he let us know because I'd be very interested! I never heard any more until years later I published my autobiography, and the phone rang and the guy said, 'I've just read your book where you talk about the first V12 in the MkX. You're the bugger who passed me, and I've been waiting all these years to find out!'

Other Changes

The V12 engine went into the Series 3 E-type, which standardized the longer wheelbase previously used only on the 2+2. The two-seater coupé was dropped, leaving just a 2+2 coupé and two-seat roadster. Other changes included a new grille, and pressed-steel wheels with wider tyres covered by flared wheel arches. Judged by the standards of the time it was quite a good update, but it couldn't hide the fact that the basic design of the E-type was now ten years old, and in the time the E-type had been on sale, American rivals such as the Mustang, Camaro and Corvette had all had major reworks. None of them could match the smoothness of the E-type's engine or the quality of its ride and handling, but headline power figures sold fast cars, and even with the V12 the E-type lagged behind.

E-Type Production Ends

The end came in 1974 when Jaguar finally stopped E-type production, ending the run with a batch of fifty Commemorative edition roadsters in black (actually one was green) with cinnamon leather. Even then the last few E-types took a while to sell, which was partly why Jaguar supported the efforts of the US-based Group 44 racing team and driver Bob Tullius with a V12 E-type in the SCCA National Championships, which Tullius won in 1975.

In its final V12 form the E-type had become a different car, more of a fast grand touring machine than a sports car. But

for the greater part of its career the E-type had been the archetypal sports car – impossibly fast and stunningly beautiful, and yet still almost within reach of the common man. The E-type was seen as the height of automotive glamour and the epitome of the Swinging Sixties, an idea reinforced by its appearances on screen in popular shows such as *The Avengers, Man in a Suitcase* and *The Persuaders*. Production company ITC wanted a white E-type for Roger Moore to drive in *The Saint*, but inexplicably Jaguar turned down the offer. The car Simon Templar ended up with, the Volvo P1800, is well known for its association with the show even today.

But perhaps the E-type didn't need that kind of promotion. It was the kind of car everyone aspired to own in the 1960s, and was genuinely an automotive icon. Taking the decision to kill it off by the time it was clearly past its best in the early 1970s was a big decision for Jaguar to make, though one made easier by falling sales – particularly in the important US market. The next big decision was how to replace it.

RESTYLING THE E-TYPE

There had been some efforts outside Jaguar to modify the E-type's appearance – despite its reputation as a strikingly good-looking car. One of the first to take on the tricky task of restyling the E-type was Pietro Frua, who was commissioned by Jaguar dealer and racer John Coombs to create a special E-type that could be made and sold in small numbers. The most significant change was a shortened nose, with a new grille and big chrome bumpers. Coombs displayed the car at the London motor show in 1966, but none were sold.

Raymond Loewy's E-type

Raymond Loewy, the industrial designer who created the Greyhound bus, the Shell logo, Concorde interiors and the livery for Air Force One, among many other projects, restyled his own E-type in 1966. Loewy had rebodied an XK140 in the mid-1950s, but the resulting car had none of the grace of the original. For the E-type he shortened the front and rear overhangs, added a new grille and quad headlamps at the front, and sunk Chevrolet Corvair lights into the tail. A glassfibre spoiler was added above a larger rear window, and there were new, tapering side windows. The considerable body modifications were carried out by French coachbuilders Pichon-Parat.

Raymond Loewy restyled his E-type but the result was distinctive, rather than beautiful.
MICHAEL GULETT

Loewy's reworked E-type had recessed rear lights, a roof spoiler, reshaped side windows and a bigger rear screen.
MICHAEL GULETT

The result was rather ill-proportioned and fussy. It seems Loewy had considerable trouble with the car, describing it in a letter to Dean Batchelor of *Road & Track* magazine as 'a catastrophic piece of junk', which had cost him $3,200 in repairs in the year he had run it. He said the E-type had 'been in the repair shop once a week and it spoiled two vacations'.

Loewy sold the car in 1968, and it remained out of view until sold in 2011 at a Bonhams auction for £97,333.

Loewy's car wasn't the only quad-headlamp E-type. A four-headlamp front-end treatment was seen on a handful of otherwise standard E-types built for well-heeled owners in the UK in the mid-1960s, but the idea never really took off.

Loewy's E-type was
virtually standard inside.
MICHAEL GULETT

An unknown E-type restyle
attempt from the 1960s.
Rectangular headlamps were
more modern, but didn't
do anything to improve the
E-type's looks.
AUTHOR'S COLLECTION

Bertone's E-type

A much more modern design appeared in 1967. John Anstey, publisher of *The Daily Telegraph* newspaper, commissioned Bertone to restyle the E-type as a publicity stunt. Bertone started with a 4.2-litre 2+2 E-type, but despite the extra space afforded by the longer wheelbase of the donor car, the finished machine was initially a two-seater (it was later modified to add small rear seats). The body, designed by Nuccio Bertone and Marcello Gandini, was steel except for the bonnet, which was aluminium alloy and incorporated a subtly raised centre section to clear the straight-six engine's cam covers.

The Bertone Pirana was commissioned by *The Daily Telegraph* **newspaper in 1969.**

ED SUPERFON

Marcello Gandini reused ideas from the Pirana in the 1968 Lamborghini Espada.

ED SUPERFON

The Pirana interior combined Italian style and classic British Smiths gauges.

ED SUPERFON

The Pirana carried over the standard E-type engine and running gear.

ED SUPERFON

The Bertone E-type was built in five months and put on display at the 1967 Earls Court motor show. It was given the name Pirana – though the badges on the car for some reason render the name as 'Piranha'. Inside the car had new seats and a different dashboard. Many of the same styling ideas clearly went into the Lamborghini Espada production car that appeared a few months later.

William Towns' E-type

Car designer William Towns, most famous for the Aston Martin DBS and later the 'wedge' Lagonda, was another to attempt to better the Jaguar's own E-type efforts. He was commissioned by Jim Thomson to restyle the E-type after Thomson crashed his own car in 1972. Thomson was managing director of Guyson International, which made shot-blasting equipment; he was also a hillclimb champion. Towns created a new shape by sculpting clay applied to the actual car, then took glassfibre moulds from the clay, which could be used to make glassfibre panels. The panels were applied to the E-type's structure with screws and resin, and they gave the Jaguar what was by then Towns' signature style of flat surfaces and sharp edges.

Thomson's car, originally yellow but later painted red, had a tuned V12 engine with six Weber LDF carburettors, which required the addition of a power bulge on the bonnet. *Motor* magazine tested the car against a Ferrari Daytona, and preferred the E12.

Towns later converted his own blue E-type to E12 specification, though with a standard engine and no power bulge. He considered offering the conversions for sale, but the end of E-type production killed the project after just these two examples were made, and with it any chance of Towns' design being considered as a potential 'F-type'.

The Owen Sedanca

Another Jaguar special that is worthy of mention, though it is further removed from the sports car spirit of the E-type, is the Owen Sedanca. Conceived by Gerald Ronson, boss of the HR Owen dealer group, it was based on Jaguar XJ6 mechanicals and had styling by Chris Humberstone. The lines were said to have been inspired by Ronson's own Lamborghini Espada, and also had some similarities to the Ferrari 365GTC/4. The aluminium bodywork was by Williams & Pritchard.

The prototype car was unveiled in September 1973, and HR Owen took eighty orders, despite a basic price of £8,500, which was more than double that of an E-type or XJ6, though significantly cheaper than the Espada or 365GTC/4. Unfortunately the car appeared just as the early 1970s oil crisis got into its stride, and all but one of the orders were cancelled. Years later HR Owen commissioned two more cars from Panther, after which no more were made.

Guyson E12 was an E-type given an angular restyle by William Towns.
BRIAN SNELSON/CC BY 2.0

The Owen Sedanca was another attempt to build a more modern Jaguar GT.
RICHARD TOWN

The Sedanca's styling, by Chris Humberstone, was said to be inspired by the Lamborghini Espada.
RICHARD TOWN

6-cylinder or V12 engines could be specified under the low nose.
RICHARD TOWN

**Despite fine looks
the Owen Sedanca
was not a success
– only three were
ordered.**
RICHARD TOWN

THE XJ-S: E-TYPE REPLACEMENT?

In the truest sense Jaguar chose not to replace the E-type at all. A direct replacement codenamed XJ21 was proposed in the mid-1960s, to be powered by the 5.3-litre V12 or a related 90-degree V8 of 3.5 litres. XJ21 was a two-plus-two that would have been available as a fastback coupé or a convertible, the latter gaining a fixed roll-over hoop as the project progressed. Alongside XJ21 there was XJ27, a bigger GT car aimed further upmarket, and possibly a smaller sports car called XJ17 that would have used Daimler's 2.5-litre V8 and the upcoming 3.5-litre Jaguar V8.

But this ambitious range of sporting models never appeared, because Jaguar lacked the resources to develop everything it wanted to. In fact it was struggling to complete development of the vital XJ6 saloon, and it was this that eventually drove William Lyons to agree to a merger with BMC in 1966. To cut costs, non-essential programmes were axed, among them XJ17 and XJ21.

'Enter the F-type' heralded *CAR* magazine on the cover of its February 1973 issue, and inside there were exclusive details of what it called 'a 6-litre replacement for the E-type'. The rendering on the magazine cover had a lot in common with a Pininfarina proposal around that time for an XJ6 replacement, the grille and rectangular headlamps possibly influencing the front end of the XJ40 years later. *CAR* said the F-type would be a two-plus-two with squared-off lines and a family resemblance to the XJ saloon, with a rear window 'of the chopped style, with side fairings of the type made fashionable by Ferraris and copied by the Chevrolet Corvette and Lotus Europa'.

That description was clearly of another project, XJ27, which launched in 1975 as the XJ-S. Rather than tag the new car 'F-type' as *CAR* predicted, and invite comparisons with the iconic E, Jaguar pointedly made the connection with the XJ saloon on which the new machine was based. It was, perhaps, a new expression of the type of car Jaguar was trying to get the E-type to be by the end of its production run – a fast, refined GT car that could cross a continent in a day and still leave the driver feeling unstressed on arrival at the destination.

XJ-S Design

The XJ-S was based on a shortened version of the XJ6 saloon platform, carrying over its suspension front and rear – the successful independent rear-end layout complete with its inboard disc brakes, and with the addition of an anti-roll bar, and a coil-sprung double-wishbone set-up at the front. The engine was the V12 from the Series 3 E-type, now fitted with Lucas fuel injection but retaining its 5340cc capacity rather than being expanded to a full 6.0 litres as *CAR* had expected. William Lyons had officially retired from Jaguar but retained a consultative role, and helped refine the design of the XJ-S initially created by Malcolm Sayer, who had been responsible for the D-type and E-type.

OPPOSITE: **The last fifty E-types, built in 1974, were the Commemorative edition cars – all V12 roadsters, all but one in this black/cinnamon colour combination.**
JAGUAR

Bob Tullius won the SCCA National Championship in 1975, after the E-type's production run had ended.

BELOW LEFT: *CAR*'s speculative rendering of an F-type in 1973 was based on leaked details of the car that would eventually emerge as the **XJ-S**.
BAUER MEDIA

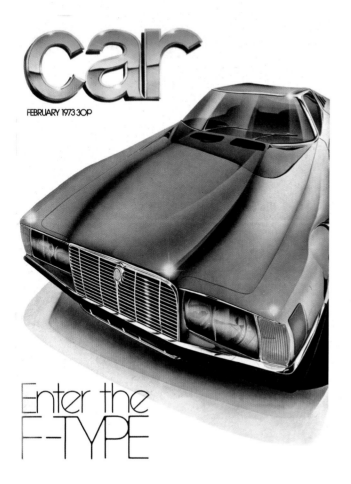

FEBRUARY 1973 30P

Enter the F-TYPE

Jaguar stylist Doug Thorpe finalized the shape, which had a few controversial elements such as the long overhangs, slot-like grille and lozenge-shaped headlamps. But nothing caused more discussion about the XJ-S than the 'flying buttress' panels swooping down from the rear corners of the roof to the back of the boot, which were said to aid aerodynamics and body stiffness. *Motor Sport* magazine said the styling had 'none of that breathtaking beauty which astounded the world on the introduction of the XK120 and the E-type'. A more forthright commentator reckoned the front, sides and rear of the XJ-S lacked harmony, and the car looked as though it had been styled by three different people – who had never met.

Inside the XJ-S there was more bad news for those who cherished traditional Jaguar values: the interior was comfortable but sparsely furnished, doing without the wood dashboard that was such a strong feature of a Jaguar saloon interior. On one level it was reasonable that the XJ-S did without wood trim, because, after all, the E-type never had it. On another, designers were seeing wood as old-fashioned and moving away from it – the Rover SD1 that was about to emerge from another arm of the British Leyland conglomerate also had a woodless interior. Whatever the designers thought, the buying public tended not to agree. XJ-S sales were slow, despite Jaguar jumping at the chance to provide cars for the television shows *Return of the Saint* and *The Avengers*.

The XJ-S took over from the E-type, but it wasn't ever really intended to be an 'F-type'.
JAGUAR

ITALIAN JAGUARS

Bertone's Ascot

Italian styling houses inevitably thought the answer was to reimagine the looks of the car completely. The first to try was Bertone, where Marcello Gandini built on the ideas seen in the Lamborghini-based Bravo in 1974 and the Ferrari-based Rainbow in 1976 to create the angular fastback Ascot. Based on an XJ-S platform shortened by about 200mm, and fitted with the usual 5.3-litre V12 engine and automatic transmission, the Ascot offered four-seat accommodation and hatchback access to its luggage space in a package that was as un-Jaguar-like as it could be.

Jaguars had always been curvy, but the Ascot's aluminium alloy bodywork seemed like a mass of straight lines and geometric shapes, with hardly a curve to be seen. Inside there were more angles, with a tall rectangular dashboard (housing a standard XJ-S instrument binnacle) and box shapes for the centre console and door furniture. Tan leather and brown suede trim reflected the aesthetic of the time.

Jaguar never seriously considered the Ascot for production, no doubt to Bertone's dismay. But in the same way that Gandini's Bertone Pirana trialled ideas that later went into the Lamborghini Espada, many of the exterior themes of the Ascot would re-emerge in another Gandini design: the 1982 Citroën BX.

Pininfarina XJ Spider

Another Italian design house, Pininfarina, had a very different approach. Unlike the angular style produced by Gandini for Bertone, Pininfarina looked back to the pure curves of the E-type for inspiration.

The Pininfarina XJ Spider that was unveiled at the first Birmingham International motor show in October 1978 was a striking blend of gentle curves, as free from fuss and adornment as the E-type had been back in 1961. More so, in fact, because modern technology allowed Pininfarina to merge the bumpers into the lines of the car. Where the E-type needed separate chrome-plated bumpers to protect the

Bertone's 1977 Ascot reimagined the XJ-S – but it was never seriously considered as a replacement for the production car.
BERTONE

29

bodywork, the XJ Spider was designed with polyurethane nose and tail sections integrated into the bodywork. That sort of thing is common now, but in 1978 it featured in only a very few production cars – Porsche's then-new 928, for example. In fact, the Spider's nose and tail sections weren't the soft plastic they were intended to be because it was too expensive to tool up for the components for a one-off: instead they were made in steel.

The XJ Spider brought back the E-type's oval air intake in the nose. It was divided internally by a horizontal bar, and flanked by wide, narrow indicators, which between them acted as a modern reminder of the early E-type's front bumpers and badge bar. Two pairs of headlamps sat in pop-up pods behind

the rear edge of the nose cone, flush with a bonnet that aped the E-type's muscular swell. The wheel arches had subtle lips in keeping with those on the Series 3 E-type, and the Spider rode on GKN alloy wheels from the donor XJ-S. The sides of the car were curved in elevation in a manner reminiscent of the E-type and D-type, and there were no exterior door handles – instead a small button was provided to unlatch the door. The body slimmed towards the middle then expanded again over the rear wheel to give the rear end a stronger look, but instead of a tapering tail to emulate the E-type there was a bold, square rear end with full-width tail lights.

Pininfarina built the car by taking a hacksaw to a pre-production XJ-S supplied to them by Jaguar, and adding the

Pininfarina's XJ Spider aimed to reintroduce some of the flowing curves of the E-type.
RAINER SCHLEGELMILCH/LAT
1017443819

The XJ Spider had a fixed roll bar to meet expected future roll-over legislation for open-top cars.
RAINER SCHLEGELMILCH/LAT
1017443819

The interior of the **XJ Spider** cocooned the two occupants in simple, leather-clad forms.
RAINER SCHLEGELMILCH/LAT 1017443788

It was intended that the **XJ Spider** would use polyurethane mouldings front and rear in place of conventional bumpers, though the concept car had steel nose and tail sections.
RAINER SCHLEGELMILCH/LAT 1017443817

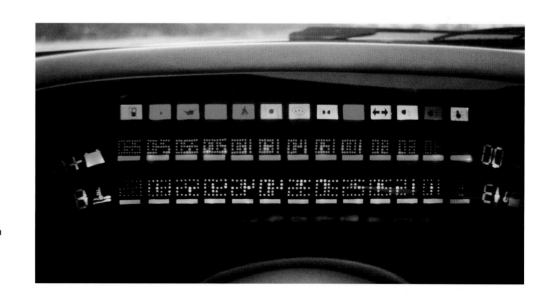

XJ Spider's digital dashboard was novel, but never likely to reach production.
RAINER SCHLEGELMILCH/LAT
1017443796

new body on top. The whole car was lower and wider than the XJ-S it was based on, and though it weighed about the same, Pininfarina's Lorenzo Ramaciotti thought a production version could be significantly lighter. Originally the Spider was painted British Racing Green, but after its show debut it was repainted in a more eye-catching silver.

As its name implied, the XJ Spider was an open car. The main part of the roof was a removable fabric panel, which clipped to the front of a fixed roll-over bar behind the front seats. Unlike the Triumph Stag, or the Reliant Scimitar GTC that would follow in a couple of years, both of which had fixed roll-over bars, there was no longitudinal member joining the roll bar to the windscreen frame. Nor did it have a fixed rear window like a Corvette: instead there was a flexible zip-out rear screen that could be rolled up and stored in the boot. The XJ Spider's roll bar was closest to that of a

Porsche 911 Targa, which also had a removable rear window in its original form.

The interior was trimmed in tan leather, with contoured seats for just two occupants. As with the exterior there was no unnecessary adornment, just simple leather-clad surfaces and a minimum of controls. The centre console carried the automatic transmission selector, electric window switches and buttons controlling a Blaupunkt radio. Behind the four-spoke Momo steering wheel there was a novel digital instrument panel with a row of red figures that lit up to show speed in kilometres per hour, and below them a row of green figures showing engine rpm.

Reaction to the XJ Spider was overwhelmingly positive. *Road & Track* splashed the Spider across the cover of its July 1979 issue, calling it 'A Dream That Could Come True', and writer Paul Frère reported that 'there is, apparently, a small chance that the car will be built'. *Motor Sport* magazine, however, said that Leyland styling boss David Bache 'held out little hope'. *CAR* magazine called it 'the Jaguar the world's been waiting for', and editor Mel Nichols declared after driving it that the XJ Spider was 'a sports car like no other... a machine with the outstanding refinement and ability of the current V12 Jaguars but with the added ingredient of fabulous looks and an open cabin'.

Nichols speculated Pininfarina could negotiate a production arrangement where Jaguar supplied the mechanical parts and Pininfarina built the cars, along the lines of the deals it already had in place with Alfa Romeo to build the 2000 Spider, with Lancia for the Monte Carlo and with Ferrari for the 400GT. 'Imagine the price Jaguar could ask for a car with such impact and such capabilities,' Nichols enthused. 'Imagine how it would look in the showrooms, and what the sales potential in the United States and such lucrative markets as Germany might be?'

But there were obstacles. Pininfarina was the first of the Italian design houses to have its own wind tunnel and routinely tested all its designs. The XJ Spider recorded a drag coefficient of 0.36 – quite good for a convertible – but had substantial front-end lift at speed. Had it been developed for production the front end of the car would have had to have been reshaped to avoid instability at the high speeds of which it would have been capable. Aerodynamic efficiency was one reason the tail of the car was high: lowering it would have improved the looks, but the car's aerodynamic performance would have been worse.

Other changes would have been necessary, too. More conventional instruments would have had to have been adopted, as Pininfarina was having second thoughts about the digital dash, and a better solution for sealing around the side windows (which overlapped the A-pillars) would have been needed to reduce noise. The prototype's seats were not adjustable, and there was no bulkhead between the cabin and the boot, which was convenient but would have been a security nightmare. The car also needed a quieter exhaust system than the modified XJ-S system used for expediency on the show car.

None of those issues was insurmountable. But Jaguar had limited resources, and bigger fish to fry: what it needed most was a world-class new saloon car to replace the ageing XJ6, which had just been given its final refresh with Pininfarina's help. Nice though the Pininfarina Spider was, it would only ever have been a short-run vehicle. So the XJ Spider never did become the F-type that so many people were looking for, and remained just a concept car – though it did influence Jaguar's future designs, as we'll see in the next chapter.

XJ-S IMPROVEMENTS

The 1970s was an era of fuel crises and rising petrol costs, and the prodigious thirst of Jaguar's big V12 had become somewhat of an embarrassment by the end of the decade. After *CAR* magazine proclaimed the Pininfarina XJ Spider as 'the Jaguar the world's been waiting for', a letter to the editor suggested that the world was not, in fact, waiting for another 15mpg two-seater.

The answer to the problem came in 1981 with Michael May's swirl-inducing 'Fireball' combustion chamber, which improved the V12's power output slightly, but more importantly made a big improvement to its fuel consumption. The revised V12 was part of two-pronged approach to getting the XJ-S to sell, the second part being the introduction of a cabriolet body style in the XJ-SC of 1983, at first available only with a 3.6-litre straight-six engine. If these strategies failed the XJ-S would be dropped. But sales did start to climb, and the big coupé earned a reprieve. V12 cabriolets appeared, followed by a full convertible, and the interior was given a timber-clad makeover to improve its showroom appeal.

A Return to Motor Racing

By then Jaguar had gone back into motor racing. Tom Walkinshaw Racing developed the XJ-S for touring car racing, and Walkinshaw himself won the European Touring

TWR's racing exploits improved the newly independent Jaguar company's image in the 1980s.

BELOW RIGHT: **TWR capitalized on the success of the Jaguar racing programme with a series of high-performance road cars.**

Car Championship and Spa 24-hours in 1984 in an XJ-S – earning some good publicity for the newly independent Jaguar company. In 1985 three cars were sent to Australia for the Bathurst 1000, and the XJ-S of John Goss and Armin Hahne won the race. TWR and Jaguar then moved on to the World Sportscar Championship with the Tony Southgate-designed XJR-6 Group C car in 1985. TWR Jaguars won the championship in 1987, 1988 and 1991 and added victory in the most famous race in the sports-car calendar, the Le Mans 24-hours, in 1988 and 1990.

TWR and Jaguar were also partners in JaguarSport, a joint venture that built highly tuned versions of Jaguar's production cars, the XJR 4.0 and XJR-S. The latter ultimately had a 6.0-litre V12 engine, though anyone looking carefully at the specs would have noticed it was no quicker than the first manual-gearbox XJ-S of 1975. A spin-off from the racing programme was the XJR-15, a road-going car based on the XJR-9 racer built at the JaguarSport factory at Wykham Mill in Bloxham.

The XJ220 Supercar

TWR was also responsible for taking the prototype XJ220 supercar that had been unveiled in 1988 and turning it into a production car. In the process it swapped from the (TWR-

sourced) 48-valve V12 engine and four-wheel drive of the prototype to two-wheel drive and an engine derived from the V6 of the XJR-10 racer, itself based on the V6 4V engine created for the MG Metro 6R4 rally car.

The XJ220 turned out to be a bittersweet project: Jaguar attracted orders for all 350 planned production cars, at a little over £415,000 each – making it the most expensive new car in the world. But the major changes in specification upset some buyers, and between the initial unveiling in 1988 and the start of production in 1992 the market for classic and bespoke cars had slumped, leaving speculators with a car they couldn't make a profit on. Jaguar had to take some to court to ensure they paid up, and in the end only 275 cars were built.

The Facelifted XJS

In 1992 the XJS lost its hyphen, and the mainstream engines were expanded to the 6.0-litre capacity that had so far been the preserve of the TWR-fettled XJR-S. There was also a new GM four-speed automatic, the rear brakes moved outboard, and the body was re-engineered so that it was cheaper to build. It had tidier windows, body-coloured bumpers and new rear-light clusters. XJS production finally ended in 1996.

It might have been replaced much earlier than that, and the car that replaced it might have returned Jaguar to sports cars more in the mould of the 6-cylinder E-type. And as we'll see, it might well have been called F-type...

The XJ220 was a spectacular 217mph (349km/h) supercar, but still not the F-type that Jaguar fans craved.
JAGUAR

In 1992 the facelifted XJS was revealed. Note the apparently larger rear side windows and aerodynamic wheels.
JAGUAR

Originally only available as a fixed-roof coupé, the XJS was later available as a cabriolet and a full convertible.
JAGUAR

CHAPTER TWO

FIRST THOUGHTS:
THE XJ41/42, XX AND X100

John Egan trained as a petroleum engineer and spent four years in the Middle East working for Shell, before taking a Masters degree at the London Business School. After working for General Motors he joined British Leyland in 1971, helping to turn around the Unipart spare-parts business before moving to tractor manufacturer Massey Ferguson. In April 1980 he returned to BL to take over as chief executive of Jaguar.

By then, BL was beginning to show signs of revival after a difficult decade. It had been crippled in the 1970s by a combination of economic conditions, oil crises, poor product quality and low productivity. Since the merger of the Leyland Motor Company and British Motor Holdings (which included Jaguar) in 1968, the company's management had done far too little to rid the group of internal competition and loss-making models, brands and production facilities. Too short-sighted to see the big decisions that needed to be made, or too timid to face up to them, the management of British Leyland had instead allowed it to sink further into the mire.

It did not help that government policy encouraged the founding of new factories in development areas such as Speke in Liverpool, rather than logistically more convenient locations near to existing production facilities in the

Jaguar's senior management team had the task of revitalizing the company and delivering a critical new saloon car to replace the ageing XJ. From left: Mike Beasley (manufacturing), Bob Berry (communications), Ken Edwards (personnel), John Egan (chief executive), David Fielden (quality), Neville Neal (service department), John Edwards (financial).
JAGUAR

Midlands. By 1975 the group was bankrupt, and following the publication of the Ryder Report, British Leyland was nationalized by Harold Wilson's Labour government.

In 1977 South African Michael Edwardes was appointed chairman and managing director of British Leyland, and set about the task of slimming down the group to more manageable proportions, while also reducing the power of the unions. Like BL's management, the unions representing the BL labour force had taken a dangerously short-term view: they had used their ability to disrupt operations across the BL group to dictate company policy, concentrating on avoiding immediate redundancies without seeing that they were sacrificing the long-term viability of the company – and with it the jobs of a far greater number of their members. While Edwardes' moves to stand up to the unions were backed, perhaps uneasily, by the Labour government headed by James Callaghan, he received enthusiastic support when a new Conservative administration led by Margaret Thatcher came to power in May 1979.

The strong leadership of Edwardes and the anti-union stance of the new government were two of the three factors that persuaded Egan that the Jaguar job – which some regarded as a poisoned chalice – was one that was worth doing. The third factor in Egan's decision was the success of Pininfarina's restyling job on the XJ saloon in April 1979. This, he judged, gave Jaguar a product that would sell well enough in the coming years so there would be time to complete the design of its replacement.

A NEW ENGINE: AJ6

The first thoughts about that replacement saloon, codenamed XJ40, had come as early as 1972. Originally the XJ40 was intended to carry over many of the mechanicals from the Series II XJ6, which was just about to go on sale. The V12 engine was still new and would be carried over, while the XK twin-cam six had been around for almost a quarter of a century and would be replaced by a new engine. A 60-degree V8 derivative of the V12 had been under development, but by 1972 there was talk of a 'slant six' design, which was essentially one bank of the V12. Then attention switched to an updated version of the XK, with a lightweight block and 24-valve cylinder head, but that proved to be too heavy and too expensive.

By 1976 work on derivatives of the XK and V12 engines had been abandoned, and instead a new engine was being

drawn up by a design team led by Harry Mundy. Like the V12 it was to be an all-alloy engine, and like the XK it was an in-line 6-cylinder engine in the 3.0-litre to 4.0-litre class. In 1983 a 3.6-litre twin-cam version of the new engine, known as the AJ6 (for Advanced Jaguar 6-cylinder) went into the XJ-SC, the new cabriolet version of the XJ-S.

Motor Sport's Alan Henry considered that the XJ-SC combined 'boulevard splendour and sports-car agility' in a blend that was more appealing than that of the more powerful V12 XJ-S. Henry was impressed with the refinement of the new engine, noting that it was only beyond 5,000rpm that it took on 'a rasping, slightly urgent growl'. Power was impressive too, and thanks to the XJ-SC's lighter weight it could match a V12 XJ-S in 0–60mph acceleration, though the bigger-engined car was quicker at the top end.

In *CAR* magazine Ian Fraser said the 6-cylinder was 'only a small step from making the V12 redundant in sheer performance terms', and offered a more sporting mien thanks to its manual gearbox, no longer an option on the V12. But not every review was positive. Fellow *CAR* scribe Steve Cropley considered the XJ-SC 'lacked decent development', and that the 3.6-litre AJ6 was 'rough and disappointing'.

DEVELOPING THE XJ40

Development of the new saloon's design had continued throughout the 1970s, starting with conventional three-box shapes that blended elements of the existing XJ and the car codenamed XJ27 – the XJ-S production car. At one stage there was a detour towards a five-door configuration, like the well-received Rover SD1 of 1976, but Jaguar soon returned to thoughts of a more traditional saloon car shape. BL management commissioned proposals from Bertone, ItalDesign and Pininfarina, and slowly a definitive design emerged. It bore a little resemblance to Pininfarina's restyle of the XJ6, but had crisper lines that were more fashionable in the late 1970s, and much better aerodynamic performance thanks to a smoother front end and tighter panel gaps. Four headlamps were planned for entry-level models, but the upper-echelon Jaguars and badge-engineered Daimlers received rectangular lamps, a new departure for Jaguar.

The shape was all but complete in 1979 and the XJ40 was slated for launch in 1984, but detail engineering took longer than envisaged, partly because BL had never invested much in Jaguar's engineering resources and there weren't enough people to do the job. But there had also been criticism of prototype cars at a customer clinic held on Long Island in 1984. Martin Broomer, head of product planning at the time, recalls:

> The main concern was the perceived poor quality of the XJ40's cabin. The new Jaguar's interior reflected a more contemporary design approach closer to that of the BMW 7 Series, a major departure from the traditional Jaguar wood and leather. The quality of the execution, however, failed to match its German rivals, particularly in the area of its plastic mouldings. As a result, the board decided to delay the launch and instigated a trim enhancement programme to address this major problem. It is probable that due to resource problems (Jaguar had only 300 engineers in total at this time) being encountered on the project as a whole, the interior trim issue became a tipping point for the wider project.

The XJ40 was not ready to be unveiled until the Birmingham International motor show in October 1986 – more than fourteen years after it was originally conceived. The delay was symptomatic not just of the limits to Jaguar's resources, but also of the importance of the car. It represented Jaguar's bread and butter for the next decade or more: nothing less than the survival of the brand relied on getting this car right.

And it *was* right, or so it appeared at first. *Fast Lane* echoed the feelings of many commentators when it said the launch of the XJ40 'dominated' the 1986 Birmingham International motor show, that the car had received 'almost universal acclaim' and that if it didn't win Car of the Year 'then that competition should be abandoned'. It didn't win.

CAR's Steve Cropley was one of the first to experience it from behind the wheel after spending a day in Arizona with Jaguar's test engineers a year before the car was publicly unveiled. The cars were well-used prototypes so Cropley could not draw too many conclusions, but he was convinced that the rigorous test programme would make the XJ40 durable in service. The XJ40 appeared on the cover of *CAR*'s November 1986 issue, with the heading 'The best saloon car in the world is British'. Inside, Gavin Green revealed that the XJ40 bettered its predecessor, the XJ6 Series III, which was in itself quite an achievement.

SPORTS-CAR OPPORTUNITY: XJ41 AND XJ42

Some of the glamour and youthful pizzazz had been lost from Jaguar's line-up as the E-type changed into a GT car, and was then replaced by the more sober, sophisticated XJ-S. To fill the gap left by the E-type's demise, two sports-car spin-offs from the XJ40 saloon were proposed, with the codenames XJ41 and XJ42. Product planner Martin Broomer remembers:

> The XJ40 programme was Jaguar's most important project since the XJ6 and vital to the company's future. It also required the BL board to commit to a major investment at a time of diminishing funds, competing projects from across the group, and Jaguar struggling to survive.
>
> To sweeten the pill for the BL board, the programme submission document included an opportunity to develop a sports-car range from XJ40 which, due to a high degree of component commonality, would minimize programme investment and the technical resources required for development. How much influence this had on the board's decision is difficult to say.
>
> At this point, the new sports car was envisaged as slotting in below the XJS to provide Jaguar with a much needed third model range.

The XJ40 saloon programme was the starting point for the XJ41/42 F-type.
JAGUAR

Work began on the XJ41/42 in the spring of 1980, and the concepts were presented to the BL board for initial approval in July. It wasn't long before everyone involved with these projects took to referring to them as the 'F-type'.

XJ41 was a coupé with two-plus-two seating and a 'Targa'-type roof with a lift-off panel, while XJ42 was a two-seat roadster with a conventional folding fabric roof. They were as closely related as the E-type open two-seater and fixed-head coupé had been. Both were, in turn, derived from the XJ40 to ensure that all three cars could be built in the most cost-effective way possible.

Management memos of the time confirm that the XJ41/42 was intended to be more in the mould of the E-type sports car than the XJ-S GT: 'XJ41 project parameters have been set more towards the performance sports sector than the luxury touring market. However, XJ41 will be better than direct competition in ride and refinement.'

The coupé came to be seen as an XJ-S replacement, aimed at the same buyers and with performance expected to equal the XJ-S V12 but with improved fuel economy. The roadster was positioned below the existing XJ-SC, and seen as a cheaper car with the emphasis on 'no frills' performance.

Initially it was thought that performance would be provided by the 3.6-litre 24-valve version of the new AJ6 engine, which delivered 221bhp in the XJ-SC and XJ40. But the high performance of the new C4-generation Chevrolet Corvette, which appeared in 1983, prompted the development of a 4.0-litre, 245bhp version of the AJ6 engine for the new car, which Jaguar planned to fit to US-market cars only. The engines drove the rear wheels via a choice of five-speed Getrag manual or four-speed ZF automatic gearboxes.

XJ41/42 Design

Jaguar designer Keith Helfet shaped the XJ41/42 at Jaguar's Browns Lane styling studio, creating themes in his initial sketches of spring 1980 that persisted through the project, despite considerable changes in the details. The nose was reminiscent of the Pininfarina XJ Spider, with a wide E-type-like oval air intake flanked by thin indicator lamps, which were a visual reminder of the slim chrome bumpers of the E-type. There were no conventional bumpers on the new car, which instead had a polyurethane nose cone that could withstand minor impacts without damage, as on Pininfarina's Spider.

The XJ41/42 had pop-up headlamps, but instead of the Pininfarina design's rectangular panels, which were at odds with the curves of the rest of the car, the Helfet design had oval panels concealing the lamps. Where the Pininfarina's long front overhang and tall tail emphasized the length of the car, the XJ41/42 design looked more cohesive, with shorter overhangs carrying less visual mass.

Flush glazing – another idea from the XJ Spider – hid the pillars and gave the glasshouse a clean, uncluttered look. Where the XJ Spider mimicked the E-type's narrow-track appearance, the XJ41/42 had a more satisfying relationship between the body and the wheels, for a stronger, more muscular stance.

Keith Helfet's initial concept drawings, presented to the BL board in the summer of 1980, formed the basis for a quarter-

Sir William Lyons was still consulted on new models right up to his death in 1985 and played a key role in the shaping of the XJ41/42 F-type Here, Keith Helfet (second right right) presents the second iteration of the XJ41 F-type to (from left) John Egan, Jim Randle and (far right) Lyons, at Lyons' home, Wappenbury Hall, in January 1984. It had a higher waistline, improved stance and other detail changes.
KEITH HELFET

scale clay model of the XJ41 coupé, which was used to refine the shape in 1981. The nose was changed, with the indicators becoming more teardrop-shaped, and the cutlines between the polyurethane nose and tail sections and the metalwork were reshaped. Within Jaguar there were some who felt the XJ41 design was too much a reflection of old ideas – harking back to the E-type rather too much – but Helfet was convinced it was the right thing to do. Moreover he had support from an illustrious quarter: Sir William Lyons himself.

Lyons had retired years before, but still came to Jaguar's styling studio once a week to keep an eye on new designs, and he was in favour of the curvaceous XJ41 that Helfet had penned. 'He held my hand,' Helfet recalls. 'He was effectively my boss on that project – I had the maestro.' It was to be the last project that Lyons was involved in before his death early in 1985. 'In that sense it's quite a significant car,' Helfet says.

The GRP model had see-through windows and a mock-up interior.
KEITH HELFET

Jaguar XJ41/42 'F-type' (1983)

Chassis and body	
Type	Steel monocoque chassis/body; two-door two-plus-two coupé with hatchback rear body and removable roof panels (XJ41), or two-door, two-seat convertible (XJ42)
Engine	
Location	Front engine, longitudinal
Block material	Aluminium
Head material	Aluminium alloy
Cylinders	6, in line
Cooling	Water
Lubrication	Wet sump
Bore × stroke	91 × 92mm
Capacity	3590cc
Main bearings	Seven
Valves/operation	4 valves per cylinder, twin chain-driven overhead camshafts
Compression ratio	Approximately 8.5:1
Fuel system	Fuel injection
Induction system	Naturally aspirated
Maximum power	221bhp at 5,000rpm
Maximum torque	248lb/ft (336Nm) at 4,000rpm

Transmission	Rear-wheel drive; Getrag five-speed manual gearbox or ZF four-speed automatic
Suspension and steering	
Front	Wishbones, coil springs, telescopic dampers and anti-roll bar
Rear	Lower wishbones, fixed-length drive shafts, coil springs with concentric dampers
Steering	Rack and pinion
Brakes	Front: ventilated discs
	Rear: solid discs
	Servo assisted
Dimensions	
Length	4,597mm (181in)
Width	1,854mm (73in)
Height	1,219mm approx. (48in)
Wheelbase	2,591mm (102in)
Unladen weight	1,847kg approx. (4,063lb)
Performance (target)	
Top speed	159mph (256km/h)
Acceleration	0–60mph: 6.6sec

Hartmann near Paris produced the first full-size mock-up from CAD data in 1987.
KEITH HELFET

Once the quarter-scale clay model had been approved, a full-scale clay was created, and taken to MIRA for wind-tunnel tests. This demonstrated that the XJ41 was a commendably low-drag shape, with a drag coefficient of 0.30 that compared well with the XJ-S's 0.38. But the rounded tail of the original design generated lift and instability, and to combat this the tail was given a higher top edge and cut-off shape, which provided a more defined separation point for the air flow.

While a clay model is easy to modify, a glassfibre model is much lighter and easier to move around without damage, and is much easier to fit with see-through windows for a more realistic appearance. So the next step was to make the first glassfibre model, and this was painted silver and despatched to Wappenbury Hall for feedback from Sir William Lyons, before being shipped to Los Angeles for a customer clinic in January 1983.

Although the XJ41 shape performed well in the clinic, where it was rated against existing sports cars and luxury GTs, there was still work to do on the design. A second clay model was made later in 1983 to refine some of the details of the shape. The waistline was lowered slightly, and the nose was reshaped again so it was slimmer and better defined, with a more distinct chin spoiler below the main oval air intake. The revised clay was used to make a second glassfibre model, and the new and old XJ41s were both taken to Wappenbury Hall in January 1984 for Lyons to compare. A second round of customer feedback in Los Angeles proved very favourable.

Changing Priorities

With engineering effort now concentrated on the XJ40 saloon, there was no way XJ41 would meet its planned 1986

The definitive XJ41 F-type, complete with E-type-like badge bar across the front intake. The car was well received at customer clinics.
KEITH HELFET

The XJ41's stablemate, the XJ42 F-type convertible. Both cars were well liked, but the project spiralled out of control and was eventually cancelled.
KEITH HELFET

launch date, so the programme was rescheduled for a late 1988 launch. At the same time, the performance parameters were re-examined in the light of new, faster competitors that were emerging. Porsche's 928 had been upgraded to a 306bhp, 4.7-litre V8 engine by 1984 and could crack the 0–60mph acceleration test in a fraction over 6sec, on the way to a top speed in excess of 150mph (241km/h) – this was a performance that XJ41 was not expected to match.

Jaguar was determined to make it the fastest car in its class, so that now meant an engine rethink. The 221bhp 3.6-litre and 245bhp 4.0-litre AJ6 engines that had already been planned would be retained for the launch, but now there was to be a 330–350bhp twin-turbo version of the larger engine available later in the model's life. With this engine XJ41 was expected to achieve 0–60mph in 5.9sec and a top speed of 160mph (258km/h), putting it firmly ahead of any existing or expected rivals.

Jaguar had been separated from the British Leyland group and privatized in the summer of 1984, and in the following year Jaguar's engineering staff were reorganized. An autonomous New Vehicle Concepts team was created to manage the development of new models, and as soon as NVC took over XJ41/42, the whole project was again put under the microscope, resulting in a number of key changes to the specification. The opportunity was also taken to use new CAD/CAM (computer aided design and manufacturing) techniques that were at the forefront of computer technology in the automotive industry. 'It was the first CAD/CAM whole car that we were aware of,' Keith Helfet recalls.

One of the most significant changes to the XJ41 was in the drivetrain. In NVC's view, raising the power output of the engine by adding turbochargers now demanded the adoption of four-wheel drive to ensure that the power could be deployed without excessive wheelspin. A few months earlier Jaguar might have been able to call upon the four-wheel-drive expertise of its BL counterpart Land Rover, but as a newly independent company Jaguar now had to develop a four-wheel-drive transmission for itself, and it engaged the Coventry four-wheel-drive specialist FF Developments to assist. It was a satisfying quirk of history that Tony Rolt, who founded FF Developments in 1971, had been a sports-car racer in the 1950s and won at Le Mans with Duncan Hamilton in a Jaguar C-type in 1953. The transmission that FF helped Jaguar to design used a viscous-type centre differential, with a second propshaft taking drive to the front axle. The new drivetrain was tested using wide-arched XJ-S mules powered by twin-turbo AJ6 engines.

XJ41/42 was based on the XJ40 and originally intended to sit below the XJ-S in the Jaguar range. This is the XJ42 roadster.
AUTHOR

Adding the extra hardware for four-wheel drive increased the weight of XJ41, and there was more extra weight to come. NVC's computer simulations had suggested that with the turbo engine there was too little cooling air passing through the radiator and engine bay. A bigger radiator and more under-bonnet space were needed, and that necessitated a 50mm (2in) increase in the width of the whole car. More weight was piled on when the decision was taken to build both the coupé and roadster from the same platform, which had to be stiff enough to work in roadster form, but as a result was heavier than it needed to be for the coupé. Still more extra kilos, and further delays, came in 1987 when the coupé was reworked with a hatchback rear end to improve its versatility.

The project continued to drag on. Across Jaguar's senior management there was a lack of experience of developing cars and manufacturing plant. Jaguar had too few engineers – hundreds, when Daimler-Benz and BMW had thousands – a legacy of Lyons' famed parsimony and Leyland's lack of foresight. The Jaguar board shelved a proposal for a long-wheelbase version of the XJ40 to free up some development resources for XJ41/42. There were concerns that vehicle engineering director Jim Randle was good at innovation but not so good at getting things done, and too often job priorities were skewed by personal prejudices. Randle was keen to get the XJ220 project off the ground, when the focus should have been on completing XJ41/42.

Styling revisions necessary as a result of the width increase were completed by October 1987, and the new

XJ41/42 was powered by Jaguar's new AJ6 engine. This is a normally aspirated unit, but there was also a 350bhp twin-turbo.
AUTHOR

BELOW LEFT: **There was no rear bumper on XJ41/42, just polyurethane buffers.**
AUTHOR

Keith Helfet remembers: 'It outscored all the exotic machinery that was around at the time.'

The West German coachbuilder Karmann was engaged to build three running cars: targa-roof coupés in blue and silver and a dark red convertible, known as CC1, CC2 and CC3. These were not true prototypes in the sense that their function was not to test and prove components and systems. Instead they were intended to demonstrate the concept, underlined by the designation 'CC' which stood for 'concept car'. CC1, the silver twin-turbo coupé, was in fact used for high-speed testing at Nardò, where it achieved 175mph (282km/h) with impressive stability.

It was also spotted by photographers, and pictures were soon splashed all over the motoring press: *CAR* magazine had no hesitation in describing it as an F-type and called it 'sensational', while also opining that the styling was a decade old, and looked it. *CAR* speculated that the non-turbo coupé would cost about £27,000 and would compete with the Porsche 944 (£25,991), while the convertible would cost £35,000 and the turbo car would be around £40,000 – much less than the £55,441 Porsche 928 S4, which had similar performance.

Inside Jaguar there was unease about the weight gain that the XJ41 had suffered. Alcan was already involved with the

interior was signed off by the end of the year, but there was a further set of detail revisions following a customer clinic in San Francisco in August 1988. An internal clinic the following spring where the XJ41 was rated against competitors rang alarm bells when it was ranked lowest for interior space and visibility – the boot space it offered, for example, was half that of an XJ-S. But it was rated highest for its styling, as

ABOVE LEFT: **Flush-fitting door handles kept the flanks clean.**
AUTHOR
ABOVE RIGHT: **The shape and position of the indicators was meant to mimic the quarter bumpers
on the nose of the E-type.**
AUTHOR

XJ220 project, and there were discussions about building the XJ41 from aluminium, though the idea was ultimately rejected. The four-wheel-drive system was deleted in an effort to drive the weight down, but even then the coupé was expected to weigh around 1,847kg (4,072lb), up from 1,560kg (3,439lb) when the project started – an increase of nearly 300kg (661lb) or almost 20 per cent. XJ41 was heavier than the XJS, and heavier even than the bigger, four-door XJ40 saloon. A Porsche 928, in stark contrast, weighed less than 1,600kg (3,527lb). Cost was an issue too: as the project had evolved away from its original concept, the commonality it had with the XJ40 had been eroded, and as the number of unique parts increased, so the cost rose.

In November 1989, just as Ford was preparing to buy Jaguar, the XJ41/42 project was formally handed over from the New Vehicle Concepts team to Jaguar's mainstream engineering group. There was plenty of work still to do before the car could enter production, and with resources now being diverted to the reskinned XJ saloon (the X300), the XJ41 again took a back seat in Jaguar's engineering priorities. And yet Martin Broomer said: 'There was a deep-rooted desire to keep the project alive.' Some put this refusal to see the project in its true light – unfocused and out of control – down to over-confidence, bordering on arrogance, on the

part of chief executive John Egan. In some sections of the company he was referred to disparagingly as 'John Ego'.

A damning report from sales and marketing in March 1990 summarized the long list of slippage in the XJ41/42

**The interior has Jaguar's traditional wood and leather,
but space is at a premium.**
AUTHOR

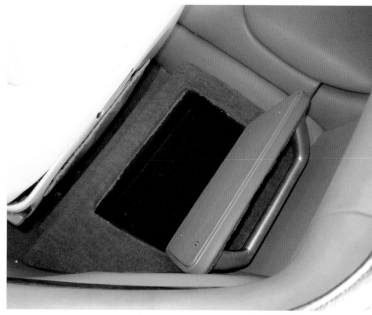

ABOVE LEFT AND RIGHT: **Small, lidded storage boxes are provided behind the seats.**
AUTHOR

Seat controls are inset into the wood trim on the door.
AUTHOR

programme, and pointed out that there were now a great many more accomplished rivals than there had been when the project began. It argued that it was too heavy and too costly, and ultimately the management of Jaguar and Ford agreed. By the end of that month XJ41 and XJ42 had been killed off by Bill Hayden, the new Jaguar managing director appointed by Ford. 'It wasn't until Ford took over that the truth of the project was finally faced up to,' Broomer says. 'I was "lucky" enough to be in the room when the decision to cancel actually happened.'

The 'Randle handle' transmission
selector familiar from the XJ40 made
a reappearance on XJ41/42.
AUTHOR

The dashboard was a mixture of existing
Jaguar components and new parts.
AUTHOR

XJ42 sits in the Gaydon
Collections Centre,
alongside dozens of other
rare Jaguars. The project was
finally cancelled by Ford in
1990.
AUTHOR

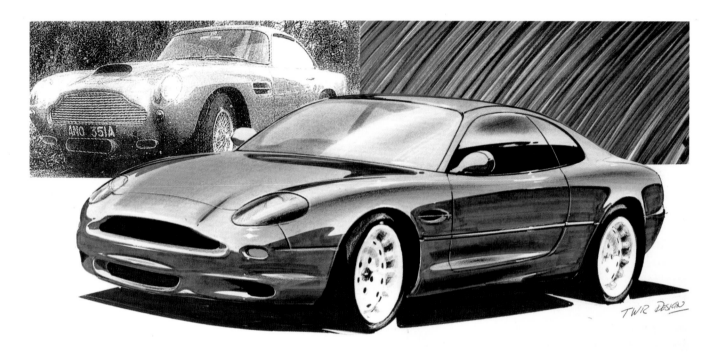

Ian Callum adapted the **XJ41**'s shape, first to fit the **XJ-S** platform and then to imbue it with a feeling of Aston-ness to create the **DB7**.

ASTON MARTIN

NPX, the Aston DB7 prototype, had an XJ41-style twin-turbo AJ6 engine – underlining the relationship with the Jaguar project.

ASTON MARTIN

Jaguar XJ41/42 'F-Type' (1989)

Chassis and body

Type	Steel monocoque chassis/body; two-door two-plus-two coupé with hatchback rear body and removable roof panels (XJ41) or two-door, two-seat convertible (XJ42)

Engine

Location	Front engine, longitudinal
Block material	Aluminium
Head material	Aluminium alloy
Cylinders	6, in line
Cooling	Water
Lubrication	Wet sump
Bore × stroke	91 × 102mm
Capacity	3980cc
Main bearings	Seven
Valves/operation	4 valves per cylinder, twin chain-driven overhead camshafts
Compression ratio	Approximately 8.5:1
Fuel system	Fuel injection
Induction system	Twin turbochargers
Maximum power	370bhp at 5,000rpm approx.
Maximum torque	400lb/ft (542Nm) at 3,000rpm approx.

Transmission

	Four-wheel drive; Getrag five-speed manual gearbox

Suspension and steering

Front	Wishbones, coil springs, telescopic dampers and anti-roll bar
Rear	Lower wishbones, fixed-length drive shafts, coil springs with concentric dampers
Steering	Rack and pinion
Brakes	Front: ventilated discs
	Rear: solid discs
	Servo assisted

Dimensions

Length	4,597mm (181in)
Width	1,854mm (73in)
Height	1,219mm approx. (48in)
Wheelbase	2,591mm (102in)
Unladen weight	1,847kg approx. (4,063lb)

Performance

Top speed	175mph (282km/h)
Acceleration	0–60mph: 5.5sec approx.

PROJECT XX

Though the long-running XJ41/42 project had finally come to a close, its story did not end there, thanks to the entrepreneurial skills of Tom Walkinshaw. Walkinshaw had been racing Jaguars since 1982 and the relationship between Jaguar and TWR, Walkinshaw's racing and vehicle engineering group, had become closer and closer. The two companies collaborated on Group C racing cars and on road-car projects such as the XJR-S, XJ220 and XJR15. As a trusted ally Walkinshaw was fully briefed on Jaguar's future model plans and was well aware of the development of XJ41/42.

When that project ended Walkinshaw came up with the idea of taking the XJ41's well-liked shape and applying it to the existing XJ-S platform – to some extent returning to the roots of the XJ41 project back in 1980. Walkinshaw's theory was that reusing the XJ-S underpinnings would save money compared to the cost of developing a new platform. TWR already knew how to get the best out of the XJ-S chassis thanks to its work on the XJR-S road cars and the championship-winning XJ-S racing cars. TWR had also developed a 48-valve version of Jaguar's V12 engine, with new twin overhead-cam cylinder heads designed by Al Melling, which had made its racing debut in 1988. Walkinshaw was keen to see a productionized version of that engine in a road car.

Ian Callum had recently arrived at TWR after a spell at Ford, and Walkinshaw consulted him over the feasibility of the idea: 'He called me in and showed me the XJ41, and said, could we put that on an XJ-S platform?'

The first job was to carry out what are called 'packaging studies', essentially to see if the body shape would fit around the 'hard points' on the platform – the areas of the structure that couldn't be moved for engineering reasons. The A-pillars were an early problem: the XJ-S has a very long bonnet and short cabin, so the A-pillar structure is a long way back.

> The first thing I'd want to do is move the screen forward. It's a very upright screen, the XJ-S. We worked all that out, we worked out the [windscreen] header point, we worked the glass planes out – these are just the basic principles of designing a car. We got that far on it and basically no further – and then Jaguar decided they didn't want the project and felt that the platform probably wasn't suitable.

Walkinshaw's plan had been to cut costs by reusing the XJ-S platform, but Ford felt the car would still be too expensive to build, making it unprofitable at the prices Jaguar could charge. So once again Jaguar's sports-car revival ground to a halt.

XX BECOMES NPX

Even the end of Project XX was not quite the end of a story that had begun back in 1980. Aston Martin, another established British car maker that had been swallowed up by Ford, wanted to build a smaller, cheaper car than its existing hand-built V8s. Aston boss Walter Hayes got wind of TWR's Project XX proposal, and its subsequent rejection by Jaguar, and was soon in talks with Walkinshaw about repurposing the design as a new Aston Martin. When news reached Jaguar that Aston Martin had taken over the promising Project XX it began to be referred to as 'Project Double Cross'…

Although Project XX had been rejected by Jaguar as too expensive to build and thus not profitable, Hayes realized that even a cheap Aston Martin would sell at a higher price, and that made Project XX viable. Walkinshaw was also quick

---

TWR/Jaguar Project XX (1990)

Chassis and body		Suspension and steering	
Type	Steel monocoque chassis/body with composite clamshell bonnet and boot lid; two-door two-plus-two coupé	Front	Double wishbones, coil springs, monotube dampers and anti-roll bar
		Rear	Double wishbones, longitudinal control arms, twin coil springs, twin monotube dampers, anti-roll bar
Engine		Steering	Rack and pinion
Location	Front engine, longitudinal	Brakes	Front: 362mm ventilated discs
Block material	Aluminium		Rear: 305mm solid discs
Head material	Aluminium alloy		Servo assisted
Cylinders	V12		
Cooling	Water		
Lubrication	Wet sump	**Dimensions**	
Bore × stroke	91 × 84mm approx.	Length	4,646mm (182.9in)
Capacity	6413cc approx.	Width	1,830mm (72in)
Main bearings	Seven	Height	1,238mm (48.7in)
Valves/operation	4 valves per cylinder, twin chain-driven overhead camshafts per bank	Wheelbase	2,591mm (102in)
		Unladen weight	1,750kg (3,850lb)
Compression ratio	n/a		
Fuel system	Fuel injection	**Performance**	
Induction system	Naturally aspirated	Top speed	182mph (293km/h)
Maximum power	475bhp at 6,000rpm	Acceleration	0–60mph: 4.8sec approx.
Maximum torque	470lb/ft (637Nm) at 4,500rpm		
Transmission	Rear-wheel drive; six-speed manual gearbox		

Note: Specifications are based on a one-off Aston Martin DB7 V12 built for Tom Walkinshaw in 1996, using the engine planned for Project XX

TOM WALKINSHAW

A tough, no-nonsense Scotsman, Tom Walkinshaw was a racing driver and automotive entrepreneur with strong connections to Jaguar in the 1980s. He started racing in the late 1960s and specialized in touring car racing in the 1970s, establishing his own team, Tom Walkinshaw Racing. TWR raced BMW 3.0CSLs, Mazda RX-7s, Rover SD1 Vitesses and, from 1982, entered the European Touring Car Championship with the Jaguar XJS. Walkinshaw himself won the ETCC in an XJS in 1984. After their retirement from European events the TWR Jaguars twice entered the famous Bathurst 1000 race in Australia, winning in 1985.

Following the success of the XJS programme, TWR developed Jaguar-powered Group C cars for the World Sports Car Championship, winning the championship in 1987, 1988 and 1991, and twice winning the Le Mans 24-hour race. TWR was also contracted by Jaguar to develop faster versions of the XJS and to turn the XJ220 concept into a production car. Both were subsequently built at TWR's own factory in Bloxham, Oxfordshire. Walkinshaw was also behind the Aston Martin DB7 project, which was built at Bloxham after XJ220 production ended.

Walkinshaw became engineering director for the Benetton F1 team in 1992 and subsequently ran the Ligier team. TWR was now involved in a wide range of road and racing projects, including touring car racers for Volvo in Europe and Holden in Australia. In 1996 Walkinshaw took over the Arrows F1 team and hired reigning world champion Damon Hill to drive in 1997, nearly resulting in the team's first Grand Prix win at the Hungarian Grand Prix. But the financial strain of running Arrows was too great, and when the team closed in 2002 it led to the break-up of Walkinshaw's now substantial TWR empire. But he soon returned to racing, rekindling his relationship with Holden in Australia under the Walkinshaw Performance banner.

Walkinshaw also found time to buy and run the Gloucester Rugby Club. He still had plenty to offer his myriad business and sporting interests, but sadly he died from complications due to cancer in 2010 at the age of sixty-four.

to point out that a ready-made, low-volume production facility was also available in the shape of TWR's Bloxham factory. Ian Callum observed:

Walter Hayes was looking for someone he could partner with for the whole thing – the design, the construction, maybe even the manufacturing, and Tom seemed ideal. He had the experience, and he also had an idea. He felt he could get more off the Jaguar platform than most people could – which is true because he'd raced it, he knew it inside out and back to front, and even had a 48-valve V12 engine to put in it. We designed it around that engine.

But Hayes had strong feelings about the specification of the new Aston, and one of the key elements he wanted was a straight-six engine – like the previous Aston DB models. The first running prototype of what would become the Aston Martin DB7 had a XJ41-spec twin-turbo Jaguar AJ6 engine, but for the production car Aston developed an AJ6-based supercharged 3.2-litre engine. Walkinshaw's 48-valve V12

never did go into a production car, though he did have one fitted to a DB7 for his own use.

Although the shape of the new Aston – codenamed NPX, for 'Newport Pagnell Experimental' – was derived from Keith Helfet's XJ41 design, it was comprehensively reworked. The difference was especially obvious at the back where the pronounced haunches, a Callum trademark, and an inverted rear window gave the car a much tauter, more athletic feel. They were themes that would resurface on the F-type Coupé two decades later.

X100: THE XK8

With the XJS nearing two decades in production a replacement was needed, and four competing designs from three different studios were built up as clay models in 1992 under a project known as X100: there were codenamed Evolutionary, Progressive, Radical and Evocative.

DB7 carried over many influences from its Jaguar heritage, including XJ-style rear suspension and a supercharged engine based on the AJ6.
ASTON MARTIN

Aston Martin DB7 (1994)

Chassis and body

Type	Steel monocoque chassis/body with composite front wings and boot lid; two-door two-plus-two coupé

Engine

Location	Front engine, longitudinal
Block material	Aluminium
Head material	Aluminium alloy
Cylinders	6, in line
Cooling	Water
Lubrication	Wet sump
Bore × stroke	91 × 83mm
Capacity	3239cc
Main bearings	Seven
Valves/operation	4 valves per cylinder, twin chain-driven overhead camshafts
Compression ratio	8.3:1
Fuel system	Fuel injection
Induction system	Eaton M90 supercharger
Maximum power	335bhp at 5,750rpm
Maximum torque	361lbft (490Nm) at 3,000rpm
Transmission	Five-speed manual gearbox; GM four-speed automatic optional; rear-wheel drive

Suspension and steering

Front	Double wishbones, coil springs, monotube dampers and anti-roll bar
Rear	Double wishbones, longitudinal control arms, twin coil springs, twin monotube dampers, anti-roll bar
Steering	Rack and pinion
Brakes	Front: 284mm ventilated discs
	Rear: 305mm solid discs
	Servo assisted

Dimensions

Length	4,646mm (182.9in)
Width	1,830mm (72in)
Height	1,238mm (48.7in)
Wheelbase	2,591mm (102in)
Unladen weight	1,725kg (3,795lb)

Performance

Top speed	165mph (266km/h)
Acceleration	0–60mph: 5.7sec

Evolutionary was styled at Ghia, Ford's in-house design studio, by Ian Callum's younger brother Moray. Based on an XJS platform, it had curvaceous window shapes, an oval grille that would reappear on the production S-type a few years later, and oval headlamps from the Mazda MX3 (Mazda was another member of the Ford family), which gave it a hint of similarity to the XJS.

Progressive was styled by the Ford design department in Dearborn under Jack Telnack, which hedged its bets by producing a clay model split down the centreline with one half carrying a Jaguar grille and the other a Mercury grille. Progressive introduced the idea of the shape of the headlamps being defined by the cutline of the bonnet.

The other two designs were created by Jaguar's own team at Whitley, led by Fergus Pollock. Radical had another version of the oval grille, flanked by elongated lamps, and a bright hoop windscreen surround similar to the one that would be seen on the 2002 Ford Thunderbird. Evocative was a better-balanced shape, which carried over some ideas from previous Jaguars, such as the oval pop-up headlamps related to the XJ220, oval wheel-arch shapes like the XJ-S, and a muscular rear arch in the style of the E-type.

Progressive and Evolutionary were quickly dismissed, while the two Whitley designs were taken forward to the next phase, which was to solicit opinions from dealers and customers over the summer of 1992. Feedback from that process went into a new design largely based on Evocative, which became known as 'A' for 'alternative'. That was developed into what became the XK8 production car, powered by a new engine, the AJ-V8, built at Ford's Bridgend engine plant. The XJS, the car that had never really been intended to be the F-type, had been replaced by another big GT that also wasn't quite in the F-type mould. But ideas for a proper sports car were not too far away.

After XJ41/42 and Project XX were rejected, Jaguar began Project X100, which became the XK8.
JAGUAR

New investment for the XK8 included the design of a new engine, the AJ-V8.
JAGUAR

Jaguar XK8

Chassis and body

Type	Steel monocoque chassis/body; two-door two-plus-two coupé, or two-door, two-seat convertible

Engine

Location	Front engine, longitudinal
Block material	Aluminium
Head material	Aluminium alloy
Cylinders	V8
Cooling	Water
Lubrication	Wet sump
Bore × stroke	86 × 86mm
Capacity	3996cc
Main bearings	Five
Valves/operation	4 valves per cylinder, twin chain-driven overhead camshafts per bank
Compression ratio	Approximately 10.7:1
Fuel system	Fuel injection
Induction system	Normally aspirated
Maximum power	290bhp at 6,100rpm
Maximum torque	290lbft (393Nm) at 4,250rpm
Transmission	Rear-wheel drive; Mercedes five-speed automatic gearbox

Suspension and steering

Front	Wishbones, coil springs, telescopic dampers and anti-roll bar
Rear	Lower wishbones, fixed-length drive shafts, coil springs with concentric dampers
Steering	Rack and pinion
Brakes	Front: ventilated discs
	Rear: ventilated discs
	Servo assisted

Dimensions

Length	4,760mm (187.4in)
Width	1,829mm (72in)
Height	1,295mm (51in)
Wheelbase	2,588mm (101.9in)
Unladen weight	1,653kg (3,644lb)

Performance

Top speed	156mph (251km/h)
Acceleration	0–60mph: 6.4sec

CHAPTER THREE

FURTHER FORWARD: THE XK180 AND F-TYPE CONCEPTS

After the demise of XJ41/42 and the subsequent replacement of the XJS with the XK8 in the mid-1990s, it looked as if Jaguar's priorities lay firmly with big GT cars and saloons. But the idea of a more sporting car to run alongside the mainstream Jaguars never went away. If anything, as the decade wore on the need for a genuine Jaguar sports car became more pressing than it had been for some time, because the sports prototype racing activities in partnership with TWR had come to an end in 1993. Jaguar needed something to keep alive its sporting heritage, and add some youthful vigour to a brand that was increasingly appealing only to middle-aged men.

The first signs of a revival in the Jaguar sports-car strain came in 1998 with a new concept car, which opened up dialogues about the kind of sports car Jaguar might be able to produce in the future – about the possibility of an F-type. For a while, that possibility looked very likely indeed.

XK180 CONCEPT (1998)

That 1998 concept car, called XK180, was built to commemorate the fiftieth anniversary of the Jaguar XK engine and to celebrate the sports cars it powered. Essentially the plan, hatched in December 1997, was to take an XKR and give it the flavour of a 1950s D-type, complete with the D's characteristic rear fin, while retaining about 75 per cent of the donor car. Jaguar advanced designer Keith Helfet – who had been responsible for the XJ41/42 and the XJ220 show car – led the design, moving quickly from computer-manipulated photos of XK8s to a full-size clay model based on a shortened XK platform. Over seven weeks in February and March 1998 the new car took shape, evolving away from the XK until it shared nothing with the donor car's exterior.

The XK8 was the basis for the XK180 concept car of 1998.
JAGUAR

The Finished Design

As well as the 125mm (5in) slice out of the wheelbase, the finished design had 110mm (4.5in) carved away from the overhang at each end, and the windscreen and A-pillars were moved back 100mm (4in). The screen was a short, double-curved plastic wind deflector, and humps behind the head-rests of the two seats aped the fairing behind the driver's head on the D-type. There was no roof, not even a folding fabric top – this was a proper roadster, and a spectacularly good-looking one.

Originally the plan had been to reveal the car at a special event with a group of VIP guests during the summer of 1998, but the success of the completed clay model encouraged

design director Geoff Lawson and Jaguar chief executive Nick Scheele to be more ambitious. They wanted a much bigger audience for the new concept, so it was decided to launch the car at the Paris motor show in November. With support from the top, the project began to develop more momentum. Lawson volunteered Helfet and his team to create a new interior for the car, which had not been in the original plan.

A New Interior

The XK180 had no door handles – to open the door you pulled a leather cord on the inside. Leather and aluminium

XK180 was built to celebrate the fiftieth anniversary of the Jaguar XK Models.
JAGUAR

Based on a shortened XK8 platform, the XK180 blended influences from Jaguar's current cars and also previous models such as the D-type and E-type.
JAGUAR

**The XK180 interior was simple
and classic.**
JAGUAR

dominated the interior, with hide-clad bucket seats and a dashboard faced in engine-turned alloy with a similar 'Spitfire wing' shape to the XK8's. Retro-styled toggle switches, machined from aluminium, and gauges with analogue faces lined up in the centre of the dash. Another alloy panel wrapped over the transmission tunnel, housing the starter button, isolator switch and the J-gate transmission selector. The left-hand side of the J-gate, which normally provided manual gear selection, was absent, and instead gearchange buttons were provided on the steering wheel. Luxury items – such as a radio and a heater – were conspicuously absent.

XK180 Engineering

On the engineering side, a shortened XKR mule was built to develop the new car's running gear and powertrain, spending hours at the handling circuit and high speed bowl at MIRA, the Motor Industry Research Association, a few miles north of Coventry. Jaguar engineers at Whitley developed a new version of the XKR's engine: the 4.0-litre supercharged AJ-V8 was tuned to improve power from the 370bhp available in the production car to a rousing 450bhp. The extra power was achieved by fitting a smaller supercharger pulley to spin the supercharger 10 per cent faster, and there was bigger

**Power came from a supercharged
4-litre AJ V8 engine.**
JAGUAR

induction pipework and a better air/water intercooler with twin water pumps. The fuel system was uprated, and there was a big-bore exhaust with no catalytic converter. As in the XKR, power was delivered to the rear wheels only via a five-speed Mercedes-sourced automatic transmission.

The running gear was substantially upgraded, with new race-style aluminium dampers and huge cross-drilled steel brake discs, 355mm in diameter at the front and 315mm at the rear, which were clamped by Brembo four-pot aluminium calipers. The five-spoke BBS wheels were the biggest rims yet seen on a Jaguar – 20in in diameter, 9in wide, with 255/35 Pirelli PZero Direzionale tyres at the front and 10in wide with 285/30 PZero Asimmetricos at the rear. (Today an

The XK180's J-gate transmission selector lost its manual gear positions and instead there were selector buttons on the steering wheel.
AUTHOR

F-type SVR has the same size front wheels, and the rears are an inch wider still.)

Jaguar's Special Vehicle Operations division at Browns Lane under the direction of Mike Massey pulled all the parts together. SVO's workshop and many of its staff had been involved in building the Daimler DS420 limousine, many of which were personalized to their buyers' requirements, so they had all the skills necessary for a bespoke project such as the XK180. Some of Jaguar's suppliers got the bug and helped create clever details, such as Valeo's LED matrix rear lights, which looked silver until they were illuminated, when they glowed red.

By early May 1998 the tooling for the aluminium bodywork was ready. The panels were made by long-time Jaguar partner Abbey Panels in Coventry, the company that had built bodies for C-types and D-types in the 1950s, and for the XJ220 earlier in the 1990s. The weight saving created by the shorter body, aluminium panels and lack of a roof – amounting to a substantial 350kg (770lb) – meant the XK180 was a much faster car than the donor XKR, which was no slouch itself. Like the XK120 of fifty years earlier, its name was based on the predicted top speed in miles per hour – but as project engineer Gary Albrighton told *CAR* magazine, it was 'a very conservative estimate'.

Paul Horrell drove the mule for *CAR* magazine, finding that the bellowing exhaust was loud enough to set off car alarms even at small throttle openings. Jaguar's engineers claimed the suspension was not yet set up properly, but according to Horrell the only flaw in its response was an unsettled feel in heavy braking. A couple of standing-start acceleration runs at MIRA with Jaguar's ride and handling guru Mike Cross at the wheel showed how quick the XK180 would be: 'On the wet track, with wheels spinning right the way through first and second gears, we get to 100mph in under 11 seconds. Blimey.'

XK180 was a roadster with no roof, and a low profile.
JAGUAR

The XK180 body was made by Abbey Panels, like that of so many previous special Jaguars.
AUTHOR

GEOFF LAWSON, JAGUAR DESIGN DIRECTOR

Geoff Lawson was design director of Jaguar for ten years from 1989, and led the design team that produced the XK180 and F-type concepts.

Lawson went to Leicester College of Art at the age of sixteen, and then to the Royal College of Art, initially as a furniture designer, but demonstrated his automotive interest at the RCA with a project on American car design. He joined General Motors in 1969 as a designer at the British GM truck brand Bedford, and later worked for GM in Europe and the USA. He moved to Jaguar in 1984 where he was responsible for the XJ220, XK8, XJ8, S-type and X-type production cars, and led a major expansion of the styling facilities at Whitley. He was a genuine car enthusiast with an exuberant personality, usually adorned with a loud tie and always with a lit cigarette in his fingers. He often commuted from his Warwickshire home to the Coventry studio in a cherry-red '69 Chevrolet Corvette.

JAGUAR

Lawson died following a stroke at the age of just fifty-four in June 1999, and was succeeded as design director by Ian Callum. Following Lawson's death, Jaguar chairman Dr Wolfgang Reitzle said he was 'an internationally respected and very popular figure, well known throughout the world's motor industry', whose great gift was the ability to recognize the importance of classic styling cues from the great Jaguars of the past and then translate them into modern Jaguars in a new and contemporary fashion.

Jaguar engineering director Mike Beasley said Lawson's talent 'sustained Jaguar's renowned design heritage and helped to establish an unprecedented product-led expansion of the company' and added that he was 'a real character ... immensely popular with all his colleagues'.

In 2000 Jaguar opened the Geoff Lawson Studio, which housed an advanced design department under the leadership of Julian Thomson.

A Show Car…

The show car was ready for paint in mid-June 1998. It was finished in dark blue, a classic colour paying tribute to the Écurie Écosse Jaguars of old, but in a modern metallic shade that had undertones of green and gold. It was a colour that would have been impossible to achieve with the paint technology of the 1950s. The car had right-hand drive, and was trimmed in beige and blue-green leather. After months of round-the-clock effort by enthusiastic designers and engineers the show car was ready for the Paris motor show. Jaguar boss Nick Scheele introduced it by saying it was 'a modern recreation of what made Jaguar famous in France and across the world, its Le Mans-winning C-types and D-types'. But later that day Scheele confirmed in a television interview that the XK180 would not go into production:

We didn't do it to get a taste, and should we, could we…? We really did it to showcase the newly reinvigorated Special Vehicle Operations, and showcase some of the technology that we'll make available downstream in other cars over the next months and years. You might just see that engine in a future vehicle. The 20in wheels and tyres, the brakes – four-pot Brembos – the suspension system, those are the kinds of things you're liable to see. And we've used the car to develop some interior trim technologies that will be helpful to us as we move into next generation projects.

Jaguar took the XK180 to Jabbeke in Belgium the following May to recreate a famous speed record set by an XK120 exactly fifty years earlier. The Ostend to Brussels motorway was regularly used for speed testing, and it was there in May 1949 that Jaguar proved that the XK120 could live up to its name by achieving 120mph (193km/h) – in fact test driver Ron 'Soapy' Sutton was timed at over 126mph (202km/h) with the car's standard windscreen and hood. With an aero screen fitted instead, the XK120 had achieved a remarkable 132.6mph (213km/h) – a record for a production-based car. For the XK180 runs the local authorities in Jabbeke closed the road, in recognition of the historic significance of the event.

At the North American International Auto Show at Detroit in January 1999, Jaguar unveiled a second XK180. Like the first one it was built at the SVO workshops in Browns Lane, this time with left-hand drive. Again it was painted dark blue, though a different shade to the original car, and there were detail changes to the lower body. The wheels were again five-spoke BBS alloys, but now of a new design. This time the interior was trimmed in tan leather.

Ian Norris drove the original car at Le Mans for the US magazine *Road & Track* and came away impressed with its ability as a high-speed tourer, with a smooth ride and stable cornering. He noted that there were two distinct elements to the noise the car made: the whine of the supercharger up

Two XK180s were built – one left-hand drive, one right-hand drive.
JAGUAR

XK180 at Silverstone with one of the cars that inspired it, the D-type.
JAGUAR

front, and the bellowing exhaust behind. The XK180 was so good, Norris said, it was a shame Jaguar would not be making any more.

...BUT not a Production Reality

Because despite the further development of the XK180, more column inches about how great it looked, and plenty of speculation that this was a machine that could, and should, go into production, it would go no further. The car that Geoff Lawson had once described as a 'Jaguar Viper' – referencing Chrysler's wild, one-off show car that became a hair-raising production sports car – never did become a production reality. But though it did not become a new F-type, it did make enough of an impression for XJS and XK-based replicas to be built, and it heavily influenced a second concept car that arrived a year later.

Jaguar XK180 (1998)

Chassis and body			*Suspension and steering*	
Type	Steel platform chassis, aluminium body; two-door two-seat roadster		Front	Double wishbones, coil springs, aluminium telescopic dampers and anti-roll bar
			Rear	Lower wishbone and fixed-length driveshaft, coil springs, aluminium telescopic dampers and anti-roll bar
Engine				
Location	Front engine, longitudinal			
Block material	Aluminium alloy		Steering	Rack and pinion, variable hydraulic assistance
Head material	Aluminium alloy			
Cylinders	V8		Brakes	Front: 356mm ventilated discs
Cooling	Water			Rear: 315mm ventilated discs
Lubrication	Wet sump			Servo assisted
Bore × stroke	86 × 86mm			
Capacity	3996cc			
Main bearings	Five		*Dimensions*	
Valves/operation	4 valves per cylinder, twin chain-driven overhead camshafts per cylinder bank		Length	4,417mm (173.9in)
			Width	1,821mm (71.7in)
Compression ratio	9.0:1		Height	1,296mm (51in)
Fuel system	Fuel injection		Wheelbase	2,461mm (96.9in)
Induction system	Supercharged		Unladen weight	1,565kg (3,450lb)
Maximum power	450bhp (456PS) at 6,150rpm			
Maximum torque	445lb/ft (460Nm)		*Performance*	
Transmission	Rear-wheel drive; Mercedes five-speed automatic transmission with steering-wheel buttons		Top speed	Over 180mph (290km/h)
			Acceleration	0–60mph: 4.5sec approx.

THE F-TYPE CONCEPT (2000)

In the spring of 1999 Helfet and his team – Briton Adam Hatton and Finn Pasi Pennaanen – were directed to start work on another concept car which had a remit focused firmly on creating a dialogue about future Jaguar sports cars. There were few constraints, apart from time: the concept had to be ready for the Detroit motor show, only eight months away.

referred to inside Jaguar as the F-type or 'the roadster' – was smaller again. A couple more inches were taken out of the wheelbase, and substantial chunks from the overhangs, so that it ended up 635mm (25in) shorter than the XK8, about 190mm (7.5in) shorter than the XK180 concept. It was also a significant 100mm (4in) narrower than either the XK180 or the XKR. Smaller than a Porsche Boxster, it was the smallest car anyone had put a Jaguar badge on in years.

Exterior Design

The new car was based on the well-liked XK180 body shape, but because the design team was freed from the requirement to base the car on an existing platform, they were able to make significant improvements. While the XK180 was shorter than the XK8 it was based on, the new car –

Interior Fittings

The interior further developed the ideas introduced in the XK180, with leather and machined aluminium, and classic-style rocker switches, which Helfet – no stranger to traditional British sports cars – felt were essential to get the right feel. The first clay model was complete in just eight weeks,

The 2000 F-type concept was a development of the XK180, but much modified and considerably smaller.
JAGUAR

BELOW: **The F-type concept parked next to the XK180 at the Jaguar Heritage Collections Centre at Gaydon shows just how much shorter the later car was.**
AUTHOR

and by August 1999 the car had been viewed and enthusiastically approved by Ford's CEO Jac Nasser.

The AJ-V6 Engine

Theoretically there was space for a V8 under the F-type's bonnet. Space was all there was under the bonnet as, unlike XK180, this was not a running car but simply a mock-up. That said, the show car was designed around the 3-litre AJ-V6

engine which had gone on sale in the S-type saloon in 1999, and would also power the X-type a couple of years later.

The V6 was Jaguar's version of the Ford Duratec V6 used in a variety of Ford group vehicles, notably the US Ford Taurus and the European Ford Mondeo (and also related to the V12 engine in the Aston Martin DB7 Vantage). It had an alloy block and heads like the AJ-V8, but with conventional cast-iron cylinder liners instead of the Nikasil-treated bores used on the V8 – and problems caused by poor-quality fuel meant the V8 would be redesigned with conventional liners in 2000.

The Jaguar V6 differed from the regular Ford version in its valvegear. The normal Duratec had finger followers operated by the camshaft, which in turn opened and closed the valves. In the Jaguar version there were simple bucket tappets over the top of the valve stems, operated on directly by the cam. In theory the finger follower system has less moving mass, making the engine rev more freely, but the bucket tappet system offered greater durability and cheaper manufacture. The Jaguar version certainly delivered more power, up from 204bhp in the most powerful Ford version to 232bhp in the S-type, with the peak power speed almost 1,000rpm higher.

Subsequent versions, which went into the XF in 2007, added continuously variable valve timing and a variable-length intake to increase power to 240bhp, while also broadening the spread of useful torque. Jaguar suggested the engine could be supercharged to produce in excess of 300bhp, though in the event that engine was never seen in

61

public in a supercharged form. The F-type's V6 engine was said to be mounted in conventional north-south fashion, as it was in the S-type, driving the rear wheels through a six-speed manual gearbox, possibly with a sequential change. It rode on 19in, nine-spoke alloy wheels, shod with 255/40ZR19 Pirelli PZero tyres.

Into Production

Autocar reckoned a production version could go on sale at around £40,000: at the time the XK8 coupé was £50,955 and the XKR £60,105, with the convertible versions of each one costing £7,000 more. The F-type would have been more expensive than a Mercedes-Benz SLK or Audi TT, but substantially quicker than either of them, competitive on price and performance with cars such as the Porsche Boxster 3.2S, the Lotus Esprit GT3, BMW E36 M3 and the BMW Z3 M. In V8 form it might have been a serious competitor for TVR's Griffith and Tuscan, though the worry for Jaguar might have been that it would steal sales from the XK8 and XKR.

But *Autocar* was bullish about the prospects for the F-type going into production, pointing out that the F-type was about the same width as the S-type, which could supply its double-wishbone independent suspension systems to the sports car, and that there was high demand for Boxsters, Z3s and SLKs:

> It's unthinkable that Jaguar would produce such a concept and miss the moment… it's hard to see Jaguar's marketeers

passing up this showroom draw and probable sales success when their task is to quadruple sales in the next few years.

In *CAR* Georg Kacher was clear: a production car, called F-type or possibly XK6, would be on sale by 2003, with a starting price around £30,000. Kacher said the car was 'gorgeous from every angle', and few would have disagreed with that. *CAR* reckoned it was possible that the F-type would be based on the X400, which emerged as the X-type saloon in 2002, complete with its transversely mounted V6 engine and four-wheel drive. But it's hard to see how the low and sleek roadster body could ever have worked with the tall, wide transverse engine location: the result would have ended up higher and dumpier, like a Jaguar-esque Audi TT.

The alternative was to use a new platform, which could also underpin the S-type replacement and be shared with other rear-drive mid-size saloons in the Ford family. Ford's DEW98 platform, which the existing S-type was based on, could then be replaced by a full-size architecture for the group's big saloons.

Exterior Design

There were plenty of clues that the F-type was a more serious prospect for production than the XK180 had ever been, even though it was only a mock-up. It had mirrors, for one thing, and although their location at the top of the A-pillars would have been unlikely to survive into production, at least they were there.

The F-type concept was unveiled at the Detroit show in January 2000.
JAGUAR

The tail of the final car had round lights recessed into the body.
JAGUAR

The F-type dashboard was similar to that of the XK180, but the centre console and steering wheel were different.
JAGUAR

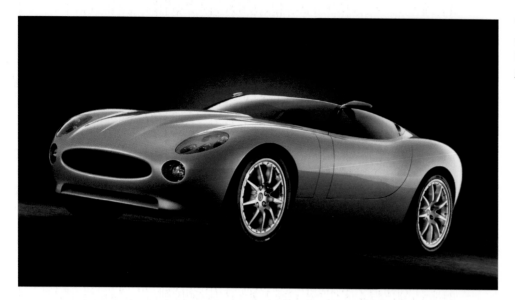

The F-type very nearly reached production – but not quite.
JAGUAR

The headlights used the latest Valeo Baroptic design, which projected the beam using a fibre-optic 'light pipe' to maximize visibility while keeping the lamps compact in size. The tail lamps were a further development of the LED clusters pioneered on the XK180. Electric door catches with hidden switches were provided. The windscreen and door windows were too low for a production car, but the screen was a conventional shape, unlike the XK180's.

There would have to be some form of bumper front and rear, but Helfet said he was well on the way to sorting out those details. In theory, at least, aerodynamic lift was taken care of with an XJ220-like underbody diffuser at the back, and a front splitter that retracted at low speed to avoid parking damage – though there hadn't been time to test the F-type in a wind tunnel.

Jaguar's new design boss Ian Callum arrived with the F-type concept well under way, and although he unveiled the car at the Detroit motor show in 2000, he readily admitted that it was the work of Helfet and his team, led by the previous design director Geoff Lawson. Jaguar released a statement from managing director Jonathan Browning explaining the thinking behind the concept:

> The F-type Concept roadster is an exercise in pure Jaguar sports-car design. Its purpose is quite simply to provoke reaction from current and potential customers. With the F-type Concept, the world is our focus group.
>
> The F-type Concept is a clear signal of Jaguar's intent to return to the true sports-car market in which we were

Intricate rear lights were a further refinement of the Valeo design produced for the XK180.
AUTHOR

so successful in the 1950s and 1960s. Complementing the recently launched S-type compact saloon, and the following year, the new X400 small saloon, the F-type Concept would attract a new generation of younger sports-car buyers, both male and female, to the Jaguar marque.

Autocar summed up what most people must have thought when the F-type broke cover in January 2000: 'It's always possible that Jaguar will not build this sports car, but that must be extremely unlikely.'

KEITH HELFET – JAGUAR DESIGNER

Keith Helfet with the XJ220: he designed the original concept car in 1988.
SILVERSTONE CLASSIC

South African-born Keith Helfet studied engineering at the University of Cape Town, but then became interested in design. His first project was a Triumph Spitfire, which he spent six months reshaping using foam and plaster of Paris. He came to the UK in 1975 to study car design at the Royal College of Art, and got a job at Jaguar three years later.

Helfet worked on the XJ40 saloon, and then the XJ41/42 'F-type', when he kept in contact with Sir William Lyons and regularly visited him at his home, Wappenbury Hall, to present styling models. He was responsible for the original XJ220 concept of 1988, the first version of what would become the XK8 production car of 1996, the XK180 concept of 1998, and the F-type concept of 2000.

He left Jaguar in 2002 to concentrate on his own company, Helfet Design, with clients in medical and industrial design. He has worked on occasional automotive projects since then, including an interesting proposal for the Morgan Aero 8, which the company chose not to pursue, and a South African electric car called the Joule.

THE F-TYPE RETURNS

There was plenty of support within Ford for the F-type, notably from chief executive Jac Nasser and design boss J. Mays. But the design worried new Jaguar design chief Ian Callum, who knew that it could lose a lot of its appeal once it had been tweaked to meet legal requirements and tweaked again to ensure production feasibility – a process that included raising the height of the windscreen, for example, and revising the bonnet line.

CAR revealed in January 2000 that a revised concept car, much closer to the production machine, based on the correct platform and fitted with the right engine, would follow early in 2001. What appeared was not quite that,

Work continued through 2000 to refine the F-type design, which changed considerably from the show car, eventually adopting a mid-engined layout.
JAGUAR

Another Adam Hatton drawing from 2000. This version of the car has a high waistline reminiscent of the BMW Z8.
JAGUAR

but instead a set of new styling sketches and an important announcement. At the Los Angeles show in January 2001 the boss of Ford's Premier Automotive Group, Dr Wolfgang Reitzle, told the press that there would be a production version of the F-type that would go on sale in 2004 or 2005. He stressed that the production car had to be affordable – both for the customer and for the company.

New sketches were released which showed that the process of refining the design had continued since the show car of a year earlier. Influences from the BMW Z8 and Porsche Boxster could be seen in some of the sketches. Despite the difference between the show car and the later sketches, and the lack of clarity over exactly what the production car would actually offer, Jaguar dealers took more than 50,000 orders from potential buyers.

The BMW Z8, which was unveiled in 1999, showing off its high waistline.

BMW

In this view the car has clear influences from the E-type, and also some similarities to the Porsche Boxster.

JAGUAR

ABOVE LEFT: **Jaguar chief executive Wolfgang Reitzle was keen on the F-type becoming a production car.**
JAGUAR

Other high-profile supporters of the 2000/1 F-type were:
ABOVE RIGHT: **Ford CEO Jacques Nasser...**
FORD

LEFT: **...and the company's design chief J. Mays.**
FORD

Jaguar F-Type (2000)

Chassis and body		Transmission	Rear-wheel drive; six-speed manual transmission with sequential change
Type	Steel monocoque chassis/body; two-door two-seat coupé		
		Suspension and steering	
Engine		Front	Double wishbones, coil springs, telescopic dampers and anti-roll bar
Location	Front engine, longitudinal		
Block material	Aluminium alloy	Rear	Double wishbones, coil springs, telescopic dampers and anti-roll bar
Head material	Aluminium alloy		
Cylinders	V6	Steering	Rack and pinion, hydraulic assistance
Cooling	Water	Brakes	Front: ventilated discs
Lubrication	Wet sump		Rear: ventilated discs
Bore × stroke	88.9 × 79.5mm		Servo assisted
Capacity	2967cc		
Main bearings	Five	*Dimensions*	
Valves/operation	4 valves per cylinder, twin chain-driven overhead camshafts per cylinder bank	Length	4,115mm (162in)
		Width	1,732mm (68.2in)
Compression ratio	10.0:1	Height	1,090mm (42.9in)
Fuel system	Fuel injection	Wheelbase	2,400mm (94.5in)
Induction system	Supercharged	Unladen weight	1,450kg (3,197lb)
Maximum power	232bhp at 6,750rpm; about 320bhp supercharged		
		Performance	
Maximum torque	220lb/ft at 4,500rpm; about 300lb/ft supercharged	Top speed	155mph (250km/h) approx.
		Acceleration	0–60mph: 5.5sec approx.

NEW DIRECTIONS: THE X600

The project to build a production car based on the F-type Concept was codenamed X600. It quickly evolved from the traditional front-engined rear-drive layout seen on the 2000 concept to a Porsche Boxster-style two-seater with an AJ-V6 engine mounted transversely behind the seats. It was said to be 'still clearly a Jaguar' despite the unfamiliar layout – Jaguar's only previous mid-engined production cars were the XJ220 and XJR15 – and the fact that it shared quite a lot under the skin with another Ford family sports car. Aston Martin, Jaguar's neighbour on the Gaydon site since 2003, was building its own small sports car codenamed AM305, and for a while the plan was for this to share a new aluminium platform with Jaguar's X600. It was also planned to use a Jaguar-based engine, though the Aston was slated for a V8 rather than the F-type's V6. Enormous design and engineering effort was put into the

X600, with more than 100 engineers working on the project at one point.

CANCELLATION OF THE F-TYPE

Gradually the optimism generated by the fine F-type shape and its rapturous reception waned, and the business case for the F-type weakened. Stock markets fell, with the end of the dot-com boom in 2000, followed by a drop in the value of telecoms companies in Europe in 2001. Economic conditions worsened in the USA and across Europe, the main potential markets for Jaguar sports cars.

Internally Jaguar had other important priorities, including the resolution of problems with the structure of the new all-aluminium X350 saloon and the development of V6

At one stage the X600 F-type might have shared a platform with the AM305 Aston Martin Vantage, and both would have been mid-engined.

ASTON MARTIN

diesel engines for the saloon cars – which were no doubt more immediately necessary, though not nearly as exciting, as building a new sports car. Engineering resources were stretched even thinner with revisions to the S-type and final work on the X-type.

In 2002 the project was mothballed, and dealers were obliged to return deposits to thousands of disappointed potential purchasers. The Aston AM305 was reworked as a front-engine/rear-drive car sharing a platform with the bigger DB9. Despite cancellation of X600, Ian Callum was adamant that Jaguar would build another sports car: 'Absolutely,' he told me when we met at Whitley in 2005. 'We've got other things to do first, but it's on the radar. It has to have the impact of the E-type, yet in a completely different way.'

FIRST LOOK: THE F-TYPE
IS LAUNCHED

Light weight has no end of benefits in car design. Downsizing and making everything lighter is a virtuous circle. Cut the weight of the body and the engine can be smaller for a given performance level, the fuel tank can be smaller because economy will improve, and the brakes and wheels smaller because the forces involved in turning and stopping are lessened. Shrinking the powertrain and running gear this way can save more weight, and so the cycle continues. Or you can take your benefits another way: lighten the car while keeping the same engine, and performance improves.

Aluminium alloys have long played a key role in lightweight vehicle design. Alloys of aluminium with copper, manganese, magnesium and other metals were developed around the same time the motor industry was gathering pace early in the twentieth century. The alloys could deliver high strength, yet the base metal's low density was retained – meaning that aluminium alloy components were light in weight. They were soon adopted by the motor industry for cast components such as gearbox casings, and replacing iron pistons with aluminium helped to increase engine speeds and raise power outputs of engines. Other alloys could be rolled and beaten into thin, light sheets that were ideal for body panels.

Using aluminium for the structure of a car was a more difficult and more costly idea that took far longer to perfect, but it would be a key technology that helped turn the F-type from a long-awaited dream to a production reality in 2012.

JAGUAR AND ALUMINIUM

Swallow and SS used aluminium alloys from the start, and in 1948 it was planned to produce the Jaguar XK120 sports car with an aluminium alloy body on top of its separate steel chassis – though in the event most XK120s had steel

X350 XJ saloon was Jaguar's first all-aluminium production car. This polished show car ensured the message of Jaguar's new technology reached the widest possible audience.
JAGUAR

bodies that could be mass-produced more cheaply and easily. Though the XK engine retained a conventional iron cylinder block, it did boast an alloy cylinder head, which saved weight and offered better heat-transfer properties. Jaguar continued to use aluminium alloy bodies on its racing machines: the C-type had alloy panels wrapped around a tubular steel frame, while the D-type extended the use of alloys, introducing a new hybrid structure with a stressed magnesium alloy tub derived from aircraft practice.

The handsome Dunlop racing wheels were also aluminium alloy. But when the E-type came along, although it had a similar method of construction, production cars were all steel, and only the rare lightweight E-type racers had substantial use of aluminium in their make-up.

The Advanced Lightweight Coupé concept of 2005 introduced aluminium construction to Jaguar's GT cars.
JAGUAR

ALC previewed the new-generation XK, and its structure would form the basis of the F-type.
JAGUAR

XK's aluminium structure was shortened to form the basis of the F-type.
JAGUAR

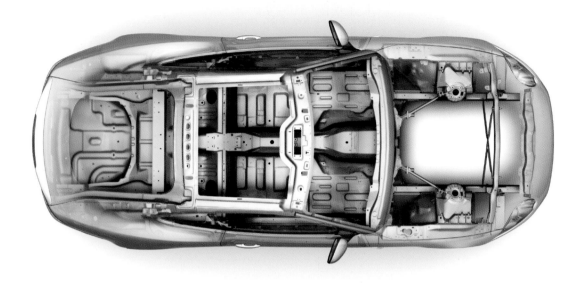

F-type's structure used the same bonded and riveted construction method as the XK and XJ.
JAGUAR

The high cost of manufacture made sure that aluminium alloy bodywork remained the preserve of high-priced exotic cars until the 1990s, when car makers chasing efficiency gains developed aluminium structures that were viable for mass production. Audi's ASF system arrived in 1994, and Jaguar's first aluminium production car was the X350 XJ saloon in 2002. When that car was launched, Jaguar claimed the aluminium alloy body was about 12 per cent lighter than a steel equivalent, and the complete car was around 90kg (200lb)

lighter than the outgoing X308 saloon, despite being a taller, wider car.

The X350 was built using a method called rivet bonding, which deployed more than 3,000 self-piercing boron steel rivets, together with aerospace-standard epoxy adhesive to construct the bodyshell from aluminium alloy castings, pressings and extrusions. Steel subframes supported the front and rear suspension. Jaguar used the same method of construction for its 2005 Advanced Lightweight Coupé concept car and the second-generation XK of 2006, which it said was 30 per cent stiffer and around 100kg (220lb) lighter than the previous steel-bodied car.

The same construction method was again used for the F-type. In fact the new car carried over much of its structure from the XK, but with the wheelbase shortened by 128mm (5in) and the overhangs trimmed by about 170mm (6.7in) as Jaguar sought to adapt a structure originally designed for a big GT to suit a medium-sized sports car. According to Jaguar the new structure weighed just 261kg (575lb).

TATA: JAGUAR'S NEW OWNERS

After years of effort and investment, Ford was forced to sell off Jaguar, Land Rover and some of its other premium brands to focus resources on other parts of its business as the recession of the late 2000s hit home. Negotiations began in June 2007 with Tata Group, an Indian multinational that owns Tata Motors, the country's largest car maker. The following March it was revealed that Tata was paying Ford £1.15 billion for the two British companies.

Ford agreed to continue supplying engines and other components for Jaguar Land Rover vehicles, including the V6 and V8 engines that would be used in the F-type.

Tata was able to take advantage of the investment Ford had made in Jaguar Land Rover's production facilities and in developing new models, among them the key Jaguar XF saloon. The company chairman, Ratan Tata, was keen for Jaguar to re-enter the sports-car market, and was an enthusiastic supporter of the F-type programme – probably more than Ford's upper hierarchy had ever been.

Rumours circulated in 2018 that Tata was considering selling Jaguar Land Rover, or discontinuing the Jaguar brand due to disappointing sales, but Tata moved swiftly to issue a statement reconfirming its commitment to both brands. In 2019 there were reports that Tata was exploring a variety of strategic options for JLR, which could include the sale of a stake in the company or the establishment of a partnership with another car maker to share development costs of new models. But analysts believed that Tata Group would not want to relinquish complete control of the company.

This F-type mule caught testing near Jaguar Land Rover's Gaydon engineering centre in December 2012 had been on the road for more than a year and was thought to have diesel power.
AUTHOR

The mule clearly shows its origins as a cut-and-shut XK. The outer exhaust pipes are dummies, and the rear bumper has been cut away to clear a prototype centre-exit F-type system.
AUTHOR

C-X16: THE F-TYPE PREVIEW

The first signs that Jaguar's continued desire for a sports car was something more solid than a vague longing came in August 2011, when the first sketch of a concept car called C-X16 was made public. The real thing followed a month later at the Frankfurt motor show, previewing the shape of the F-type production car and also introducing a fascinating new hybrid powertrain. Though that hybrid system was not carried through to the production F-type – at least it hasn't been yet – the C-X16's overall style turned out to be a clear preview of the production F-type Coupé that was still a couple of years away.

At the Frankfurt unveiling of C-X16, Jaguar brand director Adrian Hallmark explained how it fitted into the revival of the Jaguar brand. The first phase of that revival, he said, had been the renewal of Jaguar's core products – the XK, XF and XJ. That gave Jaguar, Hallmark said, 'the strongest product range on the road for several decades'. The second phase of the programme was to maximize the potential of those three model lines with new model variants and revamps. And the third stage was the introduction of breakthrough models targeting what Hallmark called 'new markets, new customers in new segments'.

The first public signs that an F-type was on the way was this sketch of the C-X16 concept released in August 2011.
JAGUAR

This sketch, by lead exterior designer Matthew Beaven, emphasized the low, tapered roofline of the C-X16.
JAGUAR

Colour rendering of the C-X16's rear three-quarter by Alex Watkin.
JAGUAR

Another Alex Watkin rendering showing the details of the E-type-inspired rear lights on the C-X16.
JAGUAR

Meanwhile the headlamps gave the car a modern, technical face.
JAGUAR

HYBRID POWER

Hallmark said that the C-X16's hybrid powertrain was the result of many years of advanced Jaguar research, and ensured that the car was 'as socially responsible as every new Jaguar must be in the future'. The C-X16 powertrain centred round a 3-litre V6 engine with 380PS (375bhp). Jaguar did not provide further details at the time, though it's clear now that this was the first application for the AJ126 V6 engine, which was derived from the AJ133 V8, and would

---

Jaguar C-X16 Concept (2011)

Chassis and body		Transmission	Rear-wheel drive; Quickshift eight-speed automatic transmission
Type	Aluminium monocoque chassis/body; two-door two-seat coupé		
		Suspension and steering	
Engine		Front	Double wishbones, coil springs, telescopic dampers and anti-roll bar
Location	Front engine, longitudinal		
Block material	Aluminium alloy	Rear	Double wishbones, coil springs, telescopic dampers and anti-roll bar
Head material	Aluminium alloy		
Cylinders	V6	Steering	Rack and pinion, electromechanical assistance
Cooling	Water		
Lubrication	Wet sump	Brakes	Discs front and rear
Bore × stroke	84.5 × 89.0mm		
Capacity	2995cc	*Dimensions*	
Main bearings	Five	Length	4,445mm (175in)
Valves/operation	4 valves per cylinder, twin chain-driven overhead camshafts per cylinder bank	Width	1,923mm (75.7in) approx.
		Height	1,297mm (51in)
Compression ratio	10.5:1	Wheelbase	2,622mm (103.2in)
Fuel system	Fuel injection	Unladen weight	1,600kg (3,527lb)
Induction system	Supercharged		
Maximum power	375bhp (380PS) at 6,500rpm plus 94bhp for 10sec	*Performance*	
		Top speed	186mph (300km/h)
Maximum torque	339lb/ft (460Nm) at 3,500–5,000rpm plus 173lb/ft (235Nm) for 10sec	Acceleration	0–60mph: 4.2sec approx.

Build of the C-X16 concept car took place at Whitley over the summer of 2011.
JAGUAR

be formally unveiled six months later at the Beijing motor show.

The V6 was the first supercharged application for Jaguar's Intelligent Stop/Start system, recently launched in the XF saloon, which could shut the engine down just 300 milliseconds after the car had come to rest. Jaguar said the twin solenoid starter could restart the engine in the time it took for the driver to move their foot from the brake to the accelerator, quicker than any competing system could manage. It was a laudable claim, though one which ignored the possibility of some Jaguar drivers being capable of left-foot braking.

To supplement the supercharged V6, C-X16 had an electric motor mounted in unit with the gearbox, drawing power from a small 1.6kWh lithium ion battery pack situated behind the seats. The battery was charged up using a kinetic energy recovery system, similar in concept to the KERS systems that had been introduced into F1 racing in 2009. In the C-X16 an electro-hydraulic system on the rear axle captured energy to charge up the battery when the car was slowing down – energy that would otherwise have been converted to heat by the brakes and then lost to the atmosphere. Both the battery pack and the electric motor were liquid cooled to ensure there was no loss of performance due to heat build-up. Battery cooling used a coolant chilled by the car's climate control system, which had an electrically driven compressor rather than an engine-driven unit to reduce losses.

The battery's energy could be released through the electric motor when the driver pressed a 'push to pass' button on the steering wheel, giving an instantaneous boost equivalent to 94bhp (74kW) of power and 173lb/ft (235Nm) of torque for up to 10sec. Jaguar said the C-X16 was capable of 0–62mph in 4.4sec, which was half a second quicker than the production V6 S F-type that was to come a year later, and it was virtually as quick as the V8 S. It could complete Jaguar's 50–70mph (80–113km/h) 'overtaking' test in 2.1sec – much quicker than either the V6 S (3.1sec) or V8 S (2.5sec) production F-types were destined to be. Adrian Hallmark called the overtaking performance 'exhilarating, phenomenal' and said that, 'quite simply, it redefines the performance car sector.'

And it wasn't just the C-X16's speed that was impressive: because it could capture and reuse energy that would otherwise go to waste, it was much more efficient, producing only 165g/km of CO_2 on the industry standard test. That was much less than even the base V6 F-type production car (209g/km) with its conventional powertrain would later achieve.

C-X16 DESIGN

As the C-X16 was being revealed at the Frankfurt show, Hallmark said it was 'as sensuous and appealing as any Jaguar has ever been'. Jaguar design director Ian Callum then took over to discuss its design in more detail. Callum said it was an important and hugely exciting moment for Jaguar: 'To be creating the future – the first two-seater Jaguar since…

well, you-know-what. This car gives us the opportunity to reconfirm and evolve the Jaguar design direction. At Jaguar Design we have spent the last six years restoring the vitality of this brand.'

He said the C-X16 represented the kind of car that should become the centre of the Jaguar brand, and was a vision for Jaguar's future. With that, the stage darkened so a big screen could show images of the C-X16's details and of

the car in motion, and the red dust-cover was whipped off to reveal the concept itself.

As the assembled journalists and photographers took in the sleek silver-painted concept car Callum went on:

As far as I'm concerned – as far as we're all concerned in Jaguar Design – if it isn't beautiful it isn't a Jaguar. Also, if it isn't exciting, it isn't a Jaguar. The C-X16 concept expresses

Florian Dobe's design for the C-X16 interior. Note the silver rectangle towards the back of the car: this is the exposed battery for the hybrid system.
JAGUAR

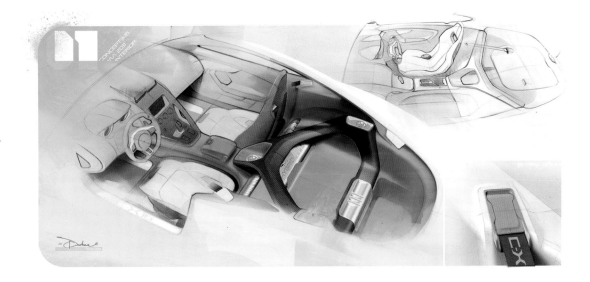

The C-X16's seats, drawn by Jonathan Sandys, were more extreme than the ones that would be seen in the F-type production cars two years later.
JAGUAR

The C-X16 steering wheel by Jonathan Sandys, showing the 'push to pass' boost button built into the rim.
JAGUAR

dynamism, it expresses vitality, and it expresses a youthful spirit. It's a sensuous design, it has cat-like agility, and it does have inspirational performance. The C-X16 delivers driver-focused performance, while inspiring an emotional connection. I want people to feel this car just has to be driven – before they even get into it.

You know, to create a sports car is actually one of the most challenging tasks of any car designer. On one hand you have to wrap the skin tightly around the car's structure and the mechanics… on the other hand, we want to create a form that's expressive and emotional, and that takes up space. The way we resolve this tension between this function and emotion is what makes Jaguar sports cars stand apart from all the others. We strive to use every millimetre to achieve that beauty of line, and, of course, that purity of form.

The C-X16, Callum explained, achieved beauty with just three key lines: the front wing feature line, the rear haunch, and the flowing roofline. All three swept towards a tail that was unfashionably low: 'This is a very powerful statement. It looks fresh, though there are unmistakable design cues that remind us this is a Jaguar – but of course we've reinterpreted them in a very modern way.'

The tail lamps, window shape and roofline were clearly related to previous Jaguars, Callum said. Most noticeable were narrow LED rear light clusters that wrapped around the corners of the car and included larger, semi-circular brake lights – the shape of them was one of the more obvious nods to the styling of the E-type. Another was the taper of the cabin in both plan and elevation, aping the E-type fixed-head coupé. At the front the C-X16 departed from the E-type and its very pure, simple oval grille: instead the new concept had an aperture

Unveiled at the Frankfurt Motor Show in 2011, C-X16 proved to be very close to the shape of the F-type production car.
JAGUAR

The side view of C-X16 would become much more familiar in 2014 with the launch of the F-type Coupé.
JAGUAR

C-X16 had a side-opening tailgate, a throwback to the E-type fixed-head coupé.
JAGUAR

with a broadly rectangular shape, which it was said represented the new face of the Jaguar brand. An oval air intake had been considered, but was rejected as too 'retro' in style.

Importantly the C-X16 had its own character, plenty of attitude and a really strong presence. The interior was seductive – and very red – and concentrated on the driver: 'It's about enveloping the driver in an architecture that's focused on control. It's about tactile technology. And because it's a Jaguar interior, it offers a sense of occasion combining premium materials, rich textures and, of course, that understated elegance.'

The C-X16, Callum concluded, demonstrated the power of the Jaguar brand and showed it at its purest.

Top Gear magazine's reaction to the C-X16 was typical: 'It's gorgeous… now the good part, it's going into production. Soon.'

WORLD TOUR

The C-X16 was back in the limelight several times as it did a round of international motor shows. In November it made

C-X16 in Delhi: now painted white, the concept poses at the 11th Auto Expo in January 2012 with (left to right) Tata Motors' Cyrus Mistry and Ravi Kant, JLR CEO Ralf Speth, Land Rover design director Gerry McGovern, Jaguar design director Ian Callum, and Tata chairman Ratan Tata.

JAGUAR

its North American debut at the Los Angeles Auto Show: the C-X16 had been silver grey when it was first seen in Frankfurt, but was repainted white for LA.

In January it appeared at the Delhi Auto Expo – an important event for Jaguar not just because it was one of the biggest motor shows in Asia, but also because its parent company, Tata Motors, was an Indian organization. It shared pride of place with the C-X75 hypercar concept.

C-X16 went on to appear at the Toronto show in February 2012, and the Beijing show that April, where it bolstered Jaguar's growing reputation in the important Chinese market.

PRODUCTION INTENT

There were hints when the C-X16 was revealed that it previewed a production car – not least from the concept itself, which was clearly a machine that would be practical to produce rather than simply a flight of fancy. Adrian Hallmark revealed that 'if' it went into production it would cost between £55,000 and £70,000. But Jaguar did not formally announce that the car would go into production – or give an indication of what it would be called – until the New York Auto Show on 4 April 2012. Making the announcement, Adrian Hallmark said:

We showed the C-X16 concept in September 2011, and the reaction to it has been so positive that we've accelerated our development of an all-new Jaguar sports car. That car will be called the F-type, and it will be unveiled in production form later this year. The core appeal of Jaguar's cars is their sporting heart, and that heart will beat more strongly than ever before in the F-type. Its development is a vivid representation of the confidence and ambition of the Jaguar brand, and the desire amongst our engineers and design team to produce a world leader in a market segment from which we have been absent for too long. But no longer – the F-type is coming.

Hallmark's words were chosen carefully to suggest that the universally positive reaction to C-X16 had encouraged Jaguar

IAN CALLUM: JAGUAR AND ASTON DB7 DESIGNER

Ian Callum studied design at the Glasgow School of Art and the Royal College of Art, then spent eleven years at Ford, contributing to image builders such as the RS200 and Escort Cosworth, as well as bread-and-butter machines such as the Fiesta and Mondeo. He also worked in Ford's Ghia studio on the Via, Zig and Zag concept cars.

In 1990 Callum left Ford to join Tom Walkinshaw's TWR group. In 2005 he explained why: 'Some of my colleagues came to see me from Ford. I'd walked away from this giant studio at Dunton, the corporation, all that stuff, into this little tin shed in Kidlington. They thought I was utterly mad. But I was as happy as could be, I was doing something I wanted to do.'

Callum shaped bodykits for TWR's tuned Mazdas and Holdens, but came to worldwide attention when TWR was commissioned to design and build the Aston Martin DB7, and Callum had the job of turning what had been a Jaguar project into a credible Aston. Callum then succeeded the late Geoff Lawson at Jaguar in 1999, taking a job he'd long dreamed of: as a youngster he wrote to Jaguar's Bill Heynes asking for a job. He immediately started asking questions about the nature of future Jaguars with the R Coupé and R-D6 concepts. In 2005 he told me: 'The next stage is to throw the rulebook away completely – because that's what Lyons would have done.' It was that sort of thinking that led to the C-X75 hybrid concept, Jaguar's first SUV, the F-Pace, and the I-Pace electric car.

Callum left Jaguar in 2019 to set up his own design company, and was succeeded as Jaguar director of design by Julian Thomson.

Jaguar design director Ian Callum was involved with TWR's rework of XJ41/42 and the F-type project of 2000–2 before leading the design of the F-type production car.
JAGUAR

to build a production version, when in truth the production F-type had been signed off long before the C-X16 was created. But the popularity of the concept would certainly have given Jaguar confidence that their new production car would be a success. When Jaguar confirmed that the F-type would launch as a convertible, it clearly signalled that a coupé, similar in profile to the C-X16 concept, would follow later. Jaguar also confirmed that there would be a range of petrol engines, including 'a new powerplant family', which would deliver 'stunning sports-car performance'.

Ian Callum, Jaguar director of design, said:

> A true sports car needs to be pure in both its purpose and its form; to have the opportunity to produce such a car for Jaguar has been a privilege both for myself and for my team. The C-type, D-type and E-type Jaguars were all sports cars that held true to this principle in their era, and the F-type will hold true to that same principle in its time, a time that is soon to arrive.

The announcement also marked the point in the F-type's development where pilot production 'final verification' prototypes built at the Castle Bromwich plant near Birmingham began testing on a variety of roads – ranging from the streets of Birmingham and Coventry to even harsher environments. This testing was intended to verify the engineering design work done in the 'virtual world', where components and assemblies are modelled on computer before any physical part is ever made.

For the F-type, more than half a million separate design analyses were carried out using ten million hours of computer processing, creating more than 300 terabytes of data – enough to fill hundreds of average computer hard drives. According to Jaguar, if that same amount of design analysis had been completed on physical cars, the number of prototype F-types that would have had to have been built would have filled the majority of the UK's motorway network (in excess of 2,000 miles/3,200km) bumper to bumper.

Ian Hoban, vehicle line director for the F-type, said:

> When you are working on a Jaguar sports car the expectations of the world are huge. We're really pleased how the attributes have translated from the virtual simulation work we've done into the physical world. Now, we're refining and adding those last few percentage points – that true element of honing that the Jaguar test team are delivering – which will turn a great sports car into an exceptional one.

DYNAMIC DEBUT

In June 2012 the F-type was seen on the move for the first time at the Goodwood Festival of Speed. It was in the safe hands of Jaguar development engineer Mike Cross. The

This prototype F-type gave the model its dynamic debut at the Goodwood Festival of Speed in 2012.
JAGUAR

At Goodwood the F-type wore camouflage made up of appropriate adjectives all beginning with F – feline, future, forward, fearless...
JAGUAR

supercharged V6 convertible was a prototype, still wearing camouflage livery, but very close to the final production specification. Goodwood arranged one of its runs to come right after a C-type, D-type and E-type had gone up the hill, to continue the sequence. Mike Cross said:

> The F-type will deliver a driver-focused sports-car experience, and camouflaged prototypes such as this one are currently being tested all over the world. The development programme is right on schedule, and coming here today to showcase just a little of the dynamic precision, noise, speed and excitement that the production F-type will exhibit is very satisfying. The reaction of the crowd has been fantastic – I'd like to keep running it up the hill all day!'

Jaguar brand director Adrian Hallmark added:

> Goodwood Festival of Speed is focused around the dynamic hill runs where the public can see, hear and smell the cars – this is why we have chosen it as the place to showcase an F-type prototype. The development programme is progressing with vigour, and we look forward to showing the world the F-type in production form later this year. When we announced

the F-type's development at New York in April of this year, we were delighted with the positive reaction from the press and public alike. The F-type will be a true sports car, so to be able to give the fans here at Goodwood a first-hand flavour of the sight and sound of Jaguar's exciting future is a great privilege.

PARIS PREMIÈRES

After the release of teaser sketches, the debut of the C-X16 concept car, the announcement that the F-type would go into production, and then its appearance on the move at Goodwood, there were still more debuts for the F-type. In Paris, at the Musée Godin on the evening of 26 September 2012, Jaguar previewed the F-type production car to a select audience. Following the reveal, singer Lana Del Rey performed a new song 'Burning Desire', which also featured in a short film *The Desire* by Ridley Scott. Both Scott's film and the video for the song heavily featured the F-type.

A day later the F-type made its global debut in definitive production form at 8am on the first press preview day of the Paris motor show. Flanked by the F-type under a red dust-cover and the new Range Rover under a blue cover, Jaguar

Lana Del Rey with the F-type: her song 'Burning Desire' was released to coincide with the launch.
JAGUAR

Land Rover's CEO Dr Ralph Speth took to the stage to begin Jaguar Land Rover's press conference:

Today is an immensely exciting and pivotal point in time for Jaguar Land Rover. We are passionate about our work, and thrilled to offer characteristic, compelling and capable new products that showcase the best of British design, engineering and manufacturing.

Speth handed over to Land Rover brand director John Edwards and design director Gerry McGovern to unveil the Range Rover, and then the stage was set for the F-type reveal. It began, appropriately enough, with the growl of a Jaguar V8 engine while images of the C-type, D-type and E-type filled massive screens in front of the waiting crowds of media.

Adrian Hallmark, global brand director for Jaguar, then took the stage:

Today is a momentous day in Jaguar history. We have already embarked on the most ambitious investment programme in the history of the company with a plan to transform the business from a niche player to a significant force in the global premium market. We have a clear vision for our future brand positioning, and we have a rich heritage – and more importantly a unique DNA defined by three strong pillars: innovative technology, seductive design, with inspirational performance. The result of these three elements is a car that feels as alive as you are.

Today I'm proud to be able to present a breakthrough product from Jaguar, the first product from this new invest-

Jaguar global brand director Adrian Hallmark introduces the F-type at its Paris motor show launch in 2012.

JAGUAR

ment strategy, and with it – after fifty years – the return to the sports-car segment.

Jaguar is a founder member of the sports-car club. Ninety years ago this month, at the age of just twenty-one, a man called William Lyons started the Jaguar story, and he moved with pace. In just over a decade he had already developed one of the most iconic and successful sports cars of its day – the SS Jaguar 100.

Following this vehicle came the XK120, the world's fastest production car, and its name denoted its predicted top speed – but of course it went faster than that. This breakthrough and its innovative spirit then flowed through into the most

successful period for Jaguar in sports cars, namely the stunning C-types and D-types – ultra-precise, ultra-lightweight, ultimately powerful and world beaters on the motorsport stage.

If this wasn't enough, he then seemed to find another gear in the gearbox. 1961 saw the birth of one of the greatest cars in automotive history – and in the opinion of many, certainly the most beautiful: the Jaguar E-type. It perfectly represented the core values of Jaguar at their pinnacle state – innovative technology, seductive design and inspirational performance. It also reframed the way the world looked at sports cars.

So imagine the challenge facing our designers and engineers when we set out to re-enter the sports-car segment: the internal challenge of honouring the bloodline and creating a spiritual successor to these automotive icons of the past, and the external challenge to surpass standards set by today's leading sports-car manufacturers. The F-type handles both of these challenges head on.

F-type is a full-blooded, full-size sports car. Its engine is at the front, its wheels are driven at the rear. Its balance is perfect. And it's a convertible. Its all-aluminium construction is extremely light and extremely rigid, and it draws on more than a decade of Jaguar's industry-leading aluminium manufacturing technology expertise. Weight distribution has been obsessively optimized to achieve this perfect balance front to rear to allow the driver to explore the limits of the F-type's performance, and their own, with absolute confidence.

Hallmark went on to describe the engine range, promising that each of the three options had its own 'distinct personality'. The entry-level choice would be a 340PS (335bhp) version of Jaguar's supercharged 3.0-litre V6. Next up was the F-type S with a 380PS (365bhp) version of the V6. 'For those people that want even more,' Hallmark said, 'we've created a range-topping F-type V8.' The F-type V8 S delivered 495PS (488bhp), and, as in its two stablemates, the engine was coupled to an eight-speed automatic transmission and incorporated stop/start technology.

With the F-type still under its dustsheet, but images of its details big on the screen behind him, Hallmark went on:

I can promise that whichever F-type you try or choose, each one is exhilarating, laser sharp, focused on the driver, and truly instinctive when you're behind the wheel. And they all fully uphold our founder's vision of creating cars that are not just machines but that feel truly alive in the hands of the driver.

The stage is set for the F-type to be revealed. Note the C-type and D-type on the screen behind Adrian Hallmark.
JAGUAR

Until now, he said, there had been two sports-car segments: compact cars such as the Mazda MX5 and Lotus Elise, and full-size sports cars such as the Mercedes SL and Jaguar's own XK. The F-type now defined a third segment:

Let me explain why. In terms of its footprint, its technology, its design values and outright performance, F-type is a full-size sports car. Yet in terms of price it sits in between these two established segments. As an example, in the UK prices will start at £58,500 for the F-type 340 horsepower version. Deliveries will begin in spring 2013. Innovative technology, seductive design, inspirational performance – and value, a combination Jaguar has always championed, and in the F-type it is stronger than ever before. This car, more than any, is the vivid signal of our future ambition. It is the essence of our

brand's DNA. And it is a testament to the world-class creativity and skills of our team.

With that, Hallmark introduced Jaguar design director Ian Callum to reveal the F-type. To prolong the tension just a little more, a short film of two F-types tackling a mountain pass played on a big screen, and as the film finished, the screen split in two to reveal two F-type convertibles, which were driven on stage. The driver of one of them was Ian Callum:

OPPOSITE: **The world's media get their first view of the F-type.**
JAGUAR

Jaguar design boss Ian Callum tells the assembled pressmen that the F-type 'speaks for itself'.
JAGUAR

BELOW: **The F-type reveal at the Paris motor show generated enormous media interest.**
JAGUAR

No other design project has given me greater pleasure than this F-type Jaguar. It's a project I've looked forward to ever since I joined the Jaguar team. It's a sports car that really is true to Jaguar's values. It's about beauty of line and purity of form. It's bold, it's confident and above all, it's desirable. The F-type is a car for now – it has its own character, it has its own time and it has its own place.

With a smile Callum concluded: 'You know I really don't need to say much else. This car speaks for itself.'

It did. The US publication *Autoweek* called it the car of the show. 'Sleek, sexy and powerful, the F-type becomes a new halo for Jaguar,' said *Autoweek*'s digital editor Andrew Stoy. 'Put the top down, fire up the engine – especially the supercharged 5.0-litre V8 – and all suddenly becomes right with the world. It's a car to covet for anyone with a love of sports cars.' In *The Daily Telegraph* Andrew English said the F-type was 'something of real worth and distinction' – though he also said that the front three-quarter view was its least appealing angle, and that it was a car for people who travelled light, as boot space was marginal.

Pistonheads said simply: 'It's got "winner" stamped all over it.'

F-TYPE DESIGN

The car's shape followed that of the C-X16 concept of 2011 – with the major exception, of course, that the production car was a convertible. The shape was defined by the 'heartlines', which formed the muscular curves of the front and rear wings. At the front the heartline began in the 'shark gills' on each side of the main grille, and led the eye upwards to the top of the front wing. The shape of the bi-xenon headlamp and thin LED daytime running lights helped to emphasize the curve, which continued over the top of the wing, back across the door and then disappeared into the rear wing. The second line then took over as the dominant visual element, sweeping over the haunch of the rear wing around into the tail.

A low, tapering tail tends to lead to rear-end lift at speed, because the shape of the body mimics the curve of an aeroplane wing. Many a sports-car design has had to be compromised by raising the tail to reduce lift, often at the expense of its appearance – notably Jaguar's XJ41/42 (*see* Chapter 2). The F-type's tail was kept low by adding an active rear spoiler, which would rise up at speed to reduce rear lift without destroying the shapely lines of the tail.

F-TYPE DETAILS

Included in the detailed information Jaguar released about the new car were key details about the aluminium structure. During the F-type's development a new, lighter aluminium front subframe had been designed, and the structure optimized for stiffness. Jaguar said the front of the F-type structure was 30 per cent stiffer than any other Jaguar. The rigidity of the structure prevented the suspension mounting points moving relative to each other under the stresses of hard cornering or on bumpy roads, preserving the integrity of the suspension geometry. In other words, the stiff F-type structure gave its suspension – aluminium double wishbones front and rear – the best chance to do its job effectively, to the benefit of the ride quality and the precision of the handling.

The interior had what Jaguar called a 'one-plus-one' layout. The asymmetric cabin was clearly built around the driver, with a grab handle on the passenger's side of the centre console providing a clear physical divide between the driver and passenger areas. There was also a subtler hint of differentiation between the two seats, with what Jaguar described as a 'more technical' finish to the trim materials on the driver's side.

Inspired by fighter-plane cockpits, the controls were grouped by function and the SportShift transmission selector was shaped like a joystick – the F-type did without the rotary gear selector of the XF and XJ. Gearshift paddles were also provided behind the steering wheel. The eight-speed ZF Quickshift automatic transmission had the same internal ratios on all three models, but a different final drive ratio depending on the engine.

A launch control function was provided on the V6 S, but curiously not on the V8. To activate it the driver selected 'Sport' mode, then held the car on the brakes with their left foot while raising the engine revs with the right. A dashboard message confirmed that launch control was ready, and when the brake was released the V6 S would deliver perfect launch.

On the F-type S and V8 S models Jaguar fitted an active exhaust system. Valves in the exhaust opened above 3,000rpm to bypass some of the silencing, reducing back pressure and giving the F-type an electrifying high-rev engine note – whichever engine was under the bonnet.

Jaguar F-type, S and V8 S Convertible (2012)

Chassis and body	
Type	Aluminium monocoque chassis/body; two-door two-seat convertible
Engine	
Location	Front engine, longitudinal
Block material	Aluminium alloy
Head material	Aluminium alloy
Cylinders	V6 or V8
Cooling	Water
Lubrication	Wet sump
Bore × stroke	V6: 84.5 × 89.0mm
	V8: 92.5 × 93.0mm
Capacity	V6: 2995cc
	V8: 5000cc
Main bearings	Five
Valves/operation	4 valves per cylinder, twin chain-driven overhead camshafts per cylinder bank
Compression ratio	V6: 10.5:1
	V8: 9.5:1
Fuel system	Fuel injection
Induction system	Supercharged
Maximum power	V6: 335bhp (340PS) at 6,500rpm
	V6 S: 375bhp (380PS) at 6,500rpm
	V8 S: 488bhp (495PS) at 6,500rpm
Maximum torque	V6: 332lbft (450Nm) at 3,500–5,000rpm
	V6 S: 339lbft (460Nm) at 3,500–5,000rpm
	V8 S: 461lbft (625Nm) at 2,500–5,500rpm

Transmission	Rear-wheel drive; Quickshift eight-speed automatic transmission
Suspension and steering	
Front	Double wishbones, coil springs, telescopic dampers and anti-roll bar
Rear	Double wishbones, coil springs, telescopic dampers and anti-roll bar
Steering	Rack and pinion, hydraulic assistance
Brakes	Front: ventilated discs, V6: 354mm, V6 S/V8 S: 380mm
	Rear: ventilated discs, V6/V6 S: 325mm, V8 S: 376mm
	Servo assisted
Dimensions	
Length	4,470mm (176in)
Width	1,923mm (75.7in)
Height	V6/V6 S: 1,296mm (51in)
	V8 S: 1,307mm (51.5in)
Wheelbase	2,622mm (103.2in)
Unladen weight	V6: 1,597kg (3,521lb)
	V6 S: 1,614kg (3,558lb)
	V8 S: 1,665kg (3,671lb)

Performance

	V6	V6 S	V8 S
Top speed	161mph (260km/h)	171mph (275km/h)	186mph (300km/h)
Acceleration	0–60mph: 5.1sec	4.8sec	4.2sec

THE V6 AND V8 ENGINES

The F-type's engines were both descended from the heavily revised version of the AJ-V8, which had first been seen in 2009. The F-type's V8 was known as AJ133 and featured a new die-cast aluminium cylinder block with cross-bolted main bearing caps to increase the stiffness of the bottom end, aiding refinement and durability. Further stiffness was added by a windage tray bolted to the bottom of the block (which also reduced oil foaming) and a hefty ribbed sump pan. Double overhead cam valve gear on each cylinder bank was supplemented by a variable valve timing system that Jaguar called Dual Independent Variable Cam Timing – or DIVCT – which helped to optimize power, torque and economy at all engine speeds.

Several car makers used variable valve timing systems, which rotated the camshaft relative to the crankshaft, advancing or retarding the timing of the valves (without changing their lift or opening duration). This change of cam phasing was done by splitting the cam-drive pulley into two layers. The outer part was driven by the cam belt or chain, and the inner part drove the camshaft. Normally the two parts were locked together so they rotated as one, but when the engine management system decided to change the phase relationship between the cam and the crankshaft to alter the valve timing, oil pressure was used to move one half of the cam pulley relative to the other.

The DIVCT system achieved the same result but without using oil pressure. Instead, it used the energy stored in the valve springs when the valves were opened to push against and rotate the camshaft relative to its drive pulley. The system could vary the cam timing very rapidly, by more than 150 degrees per second. Another benefit was that the engine's oil pump could be downsized, because oil pressure was not needed to run the system, reducing the power lost driving the pump.

Spray-guided direct injection (SGDI) delivered fuel directly into the centre of the combustion chambers at pressures of up to 300 bar (2,176PSI). Precisely measured quantities of fuel were delivered several times during each combustion cycle, improving the mixing of fuel and intake air for cleaner and more efficient combustion.

The supercharger was the latest-generation Roots-type twin vortex unit with two interlocking, twisted lobes, mounted in the V of the engine and belt-driven from the crankshaft. Compressed air from the supercharger was passed through a water-cooled intercooler to improve power and reliability. Boost was electronically managed by new Bosch engine-management software.

On its launch in 2009 in the XF, XJ and XK, the supercharged version of the V8 developed 503bhp and 461lb/ft, but in the initial F-type version the power output had dropped slightly to 488bhp, though the maximum torque figure was the same – in both engines it was limited to preserve the gearbox.

The V6 that went into the F-type had been announced at the Beijing motor show in April 2012. At that time Jaguar's mid-range engine was the AJ-V6 unit, available in 2.0-litre, 2.5-litre and 3.0-litre capacities and seen in the X-type, S-type and XF. This was a 60-degree unit based on the Ford Duratec V6, dating from the era when Ford owned Jaguar and Land Rover. But the new generation V6 engine was very different: known internally as AJ126, it was derived from the AJ133 V8 motor.

As a result the AJ126 shared the V8 engine's 90-degree bank angle, an unusual format for a V6 engine. There have been a number of 90-degree V6s in the past – Maserati's engine for the Merak and Citroën SM, the Peugeot-Renault-Volvo V6 and the Honda NSX V6 are three prominent examples, but the 90-degree V6 has also been used by Mercedes-Benz, Rover, Chrysler, Chevrolet and others. But the 90-degree bank angle results in a change to the internal balance of the engine, which is unwelcome.

All engines vibrate to some degree, but some engine configurations are better or worse than others. A V6 engine with its cylinder banks at a 60-degree angle is better balanced, and therefore smoother-running, than an in-line 4-cylinder, but not as smooth as a well-designed in-line 6. From a balance point of view a 90-degree V6 is not as good as a 60-degree unit, and to restore reasonable smoothness it needs additional rotating balance weights similar to those used on some V4 and in-line 4-cylinder engines. In the Jaguar AJ126 V6 there were rotating balance weights at the front and rear of the engine.

Why, then, move from a 60-degree V6 to a 90-degree V6 if the former is better balanced? The answer lies in the way the engines were designed and built, rather than in the details of how they performed. The AJ126 shared much of its block and head design with the V8, which meant a big saving in development time – and saving time saves money. The die-cast block, in fact, was the same length as the V8's but had new internal partitioning to blank off the unused space where the larger engine's 2 extra cylinders would have fitted.

As a result the AJ126 was not as short as it could have been – but that was no problem because every engine bay it would go into was designed to accommodate the V8 anyway. It did mean that the AJ126 was heavier than it could have been, but on the plus side it could be built on the same production line at Ford's engine plant in Bridgend as the AJ133 V8, which produced further cost savings.

The supercharged V6 had a compression ratio of 10.5:1, up from 9.5:1 in the V8, improving overall engine efficiency to reduce fuel consumption and emissions. The AJ126 had a shorter stroke and narrower bores than the V8, reducing its capacity to 2995cc. It was available in two power outputs: 340PS (335bhp) and 380PS (375bhp). Notably the two versions produced virtually the same peak torque – the 380PS engine had 339lb/ft versus 332 for the lower-output engine. This meant that the 380PS engine's performance advantage over the 340PS engine was only significant at the top of its rev range.

Early in 2013 the F-type Convertible took centre stage again at the Geneva motor show, alongside an XK120.
JAGUAR

PROMOTIONAL EVENTS

Even the launch of the F-type at the Paris show wasn't the end of the ways that Jaguar found to give the car a debut. In November 2012 the production car had its dynamic debut – the first time it was seen in public moving under its own power – at the London Lord Mayor's show. Olympic champion heptathlete Jessica Ennis, an ambassador for the Jaguar Academy of Sport, which provided bursaries to support young British sports people, drove and rode in the car, a grey F-type V6 S. The car had no registration plates, but it did not need a registration, because the roads were closed for the event.

Alongside it were two of the earliest E-types built just after the model was introduced – chassis number 4 registered 1600RW, and chassis 24 registered 1686RW, the latter a car that was given away in a *Daily Mail* competition in 1961. The three cars paraded along the route of the show proces-

sion, giving the estimated 500,000 people in the crowd, plus many thousands more watching a live BBC broadcast, the chance to see Jaguar's most famous sports car alongside its newest.

Also that month Jaguar invited three racing drivers – Martin Brundle, Justin Bell and Christian Danner – to try out the V6 S and V8 S F-types at the Snetterton race track and the surrounding Norfolk roads. Though the F-type was now a well-known shape, the cars were still carrying pre-production disguise livery. Martin Brundle, former F1 driver and winner of both the Le Mans 24-hour race and the World Sportscar Championship with the TWR Jaguar team, and more recently famous as an F1 commentator, summed up their views on the car:

A nice bark from the exhaust is the first thing you notice…
The nose goes in really well – that's probably one of the best features that I like. It's agile, it's precise, and I know that when

Jessica Ennis was on hand to give
the F-type its dynamic debut at
the London Lord Mayor's show in
November 2012.

JAGUAR

Ennis was the reigning Olympic
champion in the heptathlon,
and an ambassador for Jaguar's
Academy of Sport.

JAGUAR

I turn the wheel I'm not going to get a load of understeer with the front washing out across the road, so I can place the car exactly where I want it.

In March another racer with a significant Jaguar history, Andy Wallace, took an F-type to Belgium to recreate a famous speed test from Jaguar's past. Wallace, who won the Le Mans 24-hour race in a TWR Jaguar XJR-9 in 1988, drove a V8 S on a closed road at Jabbeke, where the XK180 had been taken fifteen years before and where the XK120 set speed records decades earlier. On a 5-mile (8km) stretch of highway, Jaguar test driver Norman Dewis had set a flying mile record of 172.4mph (277.5km/h) in a modified XK120, but Wallace had the task of trying to match that with just 2 miles (3.2km) of road to play with. In the event Wallace achieved nearly 180mph (290km/h), with the F-type still accelerating, before he had to hit the brakes to bring the car to a stop in the available distance.

Wallace's run marked the start of a convoy of Jaguar sports cars from Jabbeke to Geneva in Switzerland, where the F-type was on display on Jaguar's stand. A V8 S identical to Wallace's was driven the 519 miles (835km) to Geneva, recording an average of 35.6mpg, demonstrating the car's ability to return creditable fuel consumption for a machine with such performance potential.

Jaguar staged a ceremonial handover of F-type demonstrators to dealers all over the UK at the Ricoh Arena, home of Coventry City Football Club, in April 2013. The fifty-nine F-types were arranged in the arena car park in a giant letter F before the cars were led out for a convoy by the last E-type ever made – fittingly, as Jaguar had staged a similar event with the E-type in 1961. A line of F-types a mile and a half long and worth £4.7 million circled the infamous Coventry ring road before each car headed off to its dealer – journeys ranging

Norman Dewis (left) achieved 172mph (276.7km/h) in an XK120 at Jabbeke in 1953. Andy Wallace reached nearly 180mph (289.6km/h) there in an F-type V8 S sixty years later.
JAGUAR

BELOW: **F-types joined other Jaguar sports cars for a convoy from Jabbeke to Geneva for the motor show.**
JAGUAR

from 3.5 miles (5.6km) for Guy Salmon Jaguar in Coventry, to 440 miles (708km) for the demonstrator heading for Peter Vardy Jaguar in Aberdeen, Scotland.

In August there was another spectacular procession of Jaguar sports cars, including an F-type, this time heading into Coventry rather than out. They were there to mark the presentation of the first production F-type to Jaguar Heritage and its addition to a new Jaguar gallery at the Coventry Transport Museum. The gallery had five sections covering Jaguar's story from the 1920s to the present and future.

ABOVE: **The first fifty-nine dealer demonstrator F-types were arranged in the car park of the Coventry City football ground for a ceremonial handover in April 2013.**
JAGUAR

RIGHT: **After the giant F had been photographed from the air, the F-types were led away for a convoy along the roads around Coventry.**
JAGUAR

The F-type led a convoy of Jaguar sports cars into Coventry to mark the unveiling of a new Jaguar gallery at the Coventry Transport Museum in 2013.
JAGUAR

Ian Callum delivers the first production F-type to the new Jaguar gallery at the Coventry Transport Museum in 2013.
JAGUAR

The first production F-type went on display alongside a giant Jaguar leaper and one of the C-X75 prototypes.
AUTHOR

Union Jack-liveried F-types took to the road for a promotional tour in August 2013.
JAGUAR

Soon after, a fleet of six F-types with Union Jack liveries took part in a promotional tour of Britain, inspired by a British-themed episode of *Top Gear*, which lined up British-built vehicles on The Mall in London.

PRICES AND RIVALS

The F-type went on sale in 2013 with a base price of £58,500. The S cost £67,500 and the V8 S was £79,950. At the launch of the C-X16 the prediction had been that a production version would start at £55,000 and go up to £70,000, so the actual prices were not far off. But those prices meant that the F-type had no obvious direct rivals. It cost more than a Porsche Boxster but less than a 911. *Auto Express* compared the F-type to two potential rivals: the Audi RS5 Cabriolet, which matched the F-type S on price; and the Porsche Boxster S, which could challenge it in performance and handling. The four-seat Audi was a very different machine, and in the magazine's view it 'fails to deliver the sense of occasion you get from the F-type' – which was hardly a surprise.

The F-type was a good mix of performance, handling and ride, and was more entertaining to drive than the Audi, but for out-and-out sharpness of response it could not match the Porsche Boxster S – which was also cheaper to buy.

Generally reviews praised the F-type's looks, its aural theatre and its straight-line speed. The F-type had plenty of agility and fast, precise steering, though the Boxster was better balanced and more confidence-inspiring at the limit of adhesion. The F-type was less of a precision driving tool than a Porsche or a Lotus, and more like a Corvette with an added layer of style and civility. *Top Gear*'s Jeremy Clarkson summed it up as 'an X-rated, hardcore monster for the terminally unhinged', adding that the F-type idea was a simple one: 'Engine in the front, drive to the rear, and a big smiling piece of meat in the middle.' The biggest brickbat that reviewers had was for the F-type convertible's lack of storage space, with a tiny rear boot. The mid-engined Boxster managed to provide more luggage capacity despite its smaller overall size.

The F-type's pricing led to some interesting comparisons. Even the base V6 model was more expensive than accomplished rivals such as the BMW Z4 and Audi TT RS, while the V8 S offered performance and style competitive with more expensive cars, such as Aston Martin's V8 Vantage or the mid-engined Audi R8. As ever, the choice between them came down to what the buyer was looking for from their sports car.

CHAPTER FIVE

FURTHER DEVELOPMENTS: THE COUPÉ AND AWD

The C-X16 concept car that had previewed the F-type in 2011 teased the idea of a fastback coupé model. When the F-type production car was unveiled in 2012 it was only in convertible form, but clearly Jaguar had plans to add a hardtop version of the car to the range at some point. Fans of fixed-roof cars did not have too long to wait: the F-type Coupé appeared a year later, at the simultaneous Tokyo motor show and Los Angeles Auto Show in November 2013.

On the eve of the shows Jaguar staged a global dynamic debut event at Raleigh Studios in Playa Vista, California, with VIP guests including Simon Cowell, Miranda Kerr, David Gandy and Jody Kidd. With the arrival of the coupé came the surprise announcement of something else to excite F-type fans: a more powerful version of the V8 engine.

The most powerful F-type convertible so far was the 495PS (488bhp) V8 S, but the 5.0-litre AJ133 V8 engine that powered it was already available in a 550PS (543bhp) version in the XKR-S and XFR-S. This engine went into a new top-of-the-range F-type, the V8 R. With 11 per cent more power than the V8 S, the F-type R could accelerate significantly more swiftly: Jaguar said it could despatch the benchmark 0–60mph test in a rousing 4.0sec, while its top speed was limited to the same 186mph (300km/h) as the V8 S.

Alongside the F-type R there were two more Coupé models, with the same 380PS and 340PS V6 engines that were available in the F-type convertibles. The 495PS V8 of the most powerful convertible was not offered in the coupé.

The coupé was seen in the UK for the first time at the Jaguar Academy of Sport awards in December 2013, and the three coupé models went on sale the following spring. Jaguar designated twenty UK dealers to be R Performance Centres ready for the arrival of the F-type R coupé. The first production coupé, in Stratus Grey with 20in wheels, went to then Chelsea football manager José Mourinho.

The F-type Coupé was clearly closely related to the C-X16 concept car, as this sketch demonstrates.
JAGUAR

LEFT: **The C-X16 concept of 2011 revealed that Jaguar was thinking about a coupé F-type in addition to the convertible production car introduced in 2012.**
JAGUAR

ABOVE LEFT: **Coupé design retained the muscular rear haunches of the convertible F-type, and added a low, tapering roof.**
JAGUAR

ABOVE RIGHT: **The Coupé F-type complemented the convertible perfectly, just as the fixed-head and drophead E-types had both been fine expressions of the same theme.**
JAGUAR

RIGHT: **A spectacular event in California literally threw the spotlight on the F-type Coupé.**
JAGUAR

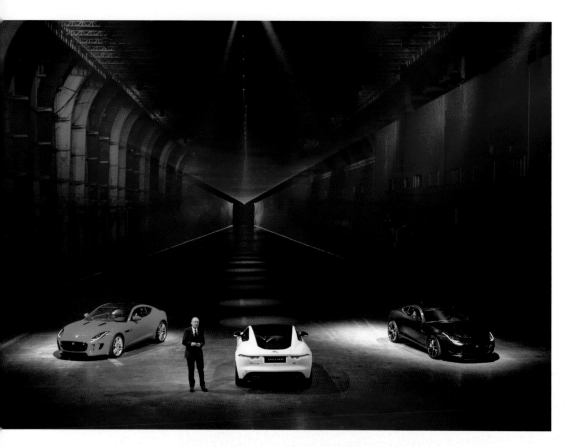

Ian Callum was on hand to talk about the design of the Coupé.
JAGUAR

Simon Cowell was one of the celebrities on hand to witness the global reveal of the F-type Coupé in 2013.
JAGUAR

ABOVE: **Model Miranda Kerr was another famous face at the global reveal of the F-type Coupé.**
JAGUAR

The F-type Coupé was unveiled to the public at the Los Angeles and Tokyo motor shows. Here the F-type R Coupé attracts media attention in Tokyo.
JAGUAR

SELLING THE F-TYPE – 'BRITISH VILLAINS' AT THE SUPER BOWL

Jaguar's 'villains': from the left, Tom Hiddleston, Sir Ben Kingsley and Mark Strong.
JAGUAR

BELOW: Jaguar's Super Bowl advertisement featured the three British actors alongside the F-type Coupé.
JAGUAR

The annual American football Super Bowl games are among the most watched television broadcasts, and an advertisement spot during the game is one of the highest-profile commercials a brand can buy. Jaguar's first came during Super Bowl XLVIII in February 2014 and prominently featured the new F-type Coupé, alongside three famous British actors.

'Have you ever noticed how in Hollywood movies, all the villains are played by Brits?' asks Sir Ben Kingsley at the start of the sixty-second advert. 'Maybe we just sound right,' intones Mark Strong, before firing up a white V8 F-type Coupé, which burbles and crackles its way through the rest of the commercial. Tom Hiddleston chases in a helicopter as the F-type races through London to what we eventually realize is a rendezvous of the three villains.

Jeff Curry of Jaguar North America explained the reasoning behind the Super Bowl advertisement spot:

Jaguar is a fast-growing luxury brand with an interesting position as a British challenger brand, and a new line-up of dynamic sports cars and sports saloon cars. Launching the F-type Coupé campaign with a Super Bowl advertisement gave us a huge platform to share our vision of British sophistication and charm to our target audience, and introduce America to the modern Jaguar brand and the all-new F-type Coupé. Our record levels of interest this past week are early indicators that Jaguar is greatly benefiting from the national exposure and social engagement that comes from participating in the Super Bowl broadcast.

The same advertisement received a repeat broadcast, this time in the UK, during another high-profile sporting event – a UEFA Champions League football match between Manchester United and Bayern Munich. A two-minute version was also screened in cinemas.

Prince Harry was one of the first to drive the F-type R Coupé, at a Goodwood track day organized by The Royal Foundation.
JAGUAR

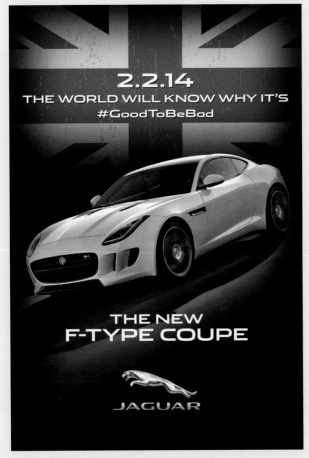

The 'villains' campaign supported the launch of the F-type Coupé.
JAGUAR

COUPÉ IN THE MEDIA

Jeremy Clarkson was typically forthright about which F-type Coupé to choose: not the base V6 'because it will make you feel a failure', and not the V8 because its electronic differential 'doesn't like being a differential or electronic' – though quite what that meant was open to question. No, Clarkson said, the best F-type was the V6 S because it delivered 'the sort of fun that makes you burst out laughing'. But he criticised the stiff suspension, a lack of visibility at angled junctions, and seats that rubbed against the bulkhead and squeaked.

CarThrottle's Alex Kersten drove the V6 S. 'This thing sounds biblical,' he said, in a video that provided plenty of evidence. 'For a 6-cylinder car this is the business. There's nothing out there that sounds quite as good. You could always go for the V8 for even more drama, but the V6 S offers all the car you would ever need.'

Road & Track noted that the coupé's body was 80 per cent stiffer than the convertible's, and on track that translated into more precise handling. Rear vision was poor, but the F-type R made up for it with its performance and shape.

Jaguar F-type, S and V8 R Coupé (2013)

Chassis and body

Type	Aluminium monocoque chassis/body; two-door two-seat coupé

Engine

Location	Front engine, longitudinal
Block material	Aluminium alloy
Head material	Aluminium alloy
Cylinders	V6 or V8
Cooling	Water
Lubrication	Wet sump
Bore × stroke	V6: 84.5 × 89.0mm
	V8: 92.5 × 93.0mm
Capacity	V6: 2995cc
	V8: 5000cc
Main bearings	Five
Valves/operation	4 valves per cylinder, twin chain-driven overhead camshafts per cylinder bank
Compression ratio	V6: 10.5:1
	V8: 9.5:1
Fuel system	Fuel injection
Induction system	Supercharged
Maximum power	V6: 335bhp (340PS) at 6,500rpm
	V6 S: 375bhp (380PS) at 6,500rpm
	V8 R: 543bhp (550PS) at 6,500rpm
Maximum torque	V6: 332lb/ft (450Nm) at 3,500–5,000rpm
	V6 S: 339lb/ft (460Nm) at 3,500–5,000rpm
	V8 R: 502lb/ft (680Nm) at 2,500–5,500rpm

Transmission

	Rear-wheel drive; Quickshift eight-speed automatic transmission

Suspension and steering

Front	Double wishbones, coil springs, telescopic dampers and anti-roll bar
Rear	Double wishbones, coil springs, telescopic dampers and anti-roll bar
Steering	Rack and pinion, hydraulic assistance
Brakes	Front: ventilated discs, V6: 354mm, V6 S/V8 R: 380mm
	Rear: ventilated discs, V6: 320mm, V6 S: 325mm, V8 R: 376mm
	Servo assisted

Dimensions

Length	4,470mm (176in)
Width	1,923mm (75.7in)
Height	V6/V6 S: 1,309mm (51.5in)
	V8 R: 1,321mm (52in)
Wheelbase	2,622mm (103.2in)
Unladen weight	V6: 1,577kg (3,477lb)
	V6 S: 1,594kg (3,514lb)
	V8 R: 1,650kg (3,638lb)

Performance

	V6	V6 S	V8 R
Top speed	162mph (261km/h)	171mph (275km/h)	186mph (300km/h)
Acceleration	0–60mph: 5.1sec	4.8sec	4.0sec

James Mills drove the coupé for the *Sunday Times* and decided the V6 cars were more nimble than the V8, though of course the F-type R was substantially swifter. It was also noisier: 'Its supercharged V8 rumbles like a thunderstorm directly overhead, shaking anyone within a hundred paces to the core. Neighbours won't thank early risers who drive to work in one of these.' Mills said the engine's huge torque could easily overwhelm the chassis, and needed care from the driver. The optional carbon ceramic brakes were a doubtful benefit as the steel brakes offered better feel and no signs of fade. Like many commentators, the *Sunday Times* identified the V6 S as the optimum model in the range.

CAR's Tim Pollard drove the V6 S Coupé, saying that the addition of a hardtop 'turned the F into a stunning piece of kit'. It was easy to live with, simple to drive around town thanks to the automatic transmission, and the 315ltr boot was a more useful size than the meagre luggage area of the convertible. The V6 S sounded great on the open road, but the exhaust's sport mode needed to be switched off entering a village to avoid sounding obnoxious. The F-type Coupé was agile, with good traction and brakes, but its responses were less sharp than a Porsche 911.

Although *CAR* thought the coupé was 'brilliant', there was criticism for the infotainment system, which looked old-fashioned compared to rivals, and buttons on the centre console that were hard to reach. Pollard said he preferred the V6 S to the F-type R as it offered a 'purer, more affordable driving experience'.

UPDATES AND ALL-WHEEL DRIVE

By the time a production car is revealed to the public, the design and engineering teams behind the scenes are already thinking about ways to improve it. With a niche model such as the F-type, extra interest is generated with limited editions and special models, as well as gradual improvements to the basic specification of the car during its production life. So it was no surprise that, not long after the launch of the original F-type convertible in 2012 and the coupé in 2013, modifications and new models began to appear.

Late in 2014 at the Los Angeles motor show Jaguar announced the 2016 model year F-types. They looked much the same as before, but underneath the skin there was big news, with the availability of four-wheel drive and manual gearboxes for the first time. Ian Hoban, vehicle line director for the F-type, explained the thinking behind the four-wheel-drive car:

Our target with engineering the all-wheel-drive F-type was to maintain that engaging rear-drive character that's so important to Jaguar sports-car DNA, yet offer even greater dynamic capability. The result is a controllable, exploitable and blisteringly fast performance car in all weather and road conditions.

In 2014 Jaguar announced that the F-type would be available with four-wheel drive.
JAGUAR

The AWD models were 100 per cent rear driven until the system sensed the rear wheels were starting to slip.
JAGUAR

A deeper bonnet bulge was a feature of the four-wheel-drive F-types.
JAGUAR

Under normal driving conditions the four-wheel-drive transmission sent 100 per cent of the engine's torque to the rear wheels to preserve the F-type's rear-driven handling feel. If the four-wheel-drive system sensed that the rear wheels were about to lose grip, it activated a centre coupling to transfer the excess torque to the front axle through a second propshaft that ran forward to the left of the gearbox and engine.

The process was controlled by a system Jaguar called Intelligent Driveline Dynamics, which connected to the engine, transmission, rear differential and the centre coupling. The system could also vary the front-to-rear torque split to improve the handling of the car, pushing torque to the front end if it sensed the onset of oversteer.

Only sharp eyes could detect the visual differences that marked out the four-wheel-drive F-types from their two-wheel-drive stablemates. The power bulge in the aluminium bonnet was now a little deeper, and there were distinctive new bonnet vents that were positioned further apart and further forward than on the rear-drive cars. The four-wheel-drive models were available with a unique 19in Volution alloy wheel design, either silver or diamond-turned grey.

The news of a manual gearbox option was music to the ears of enthusiasts who simply could not get on with the idea of a sports car with automatic transmission, which is what had been fitted to every F-type up to this point. The new gearbox had a short-travel lever with a throw of only 45mm,

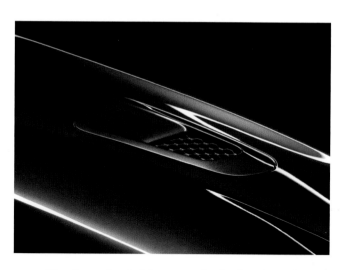

The four-wheel-drive cars also had reshaped bonnet vents.
JAGUAR

and the six forward ratios were closely stacked. Jaguar said it had placed the pedals perfectly to allow heel and toe gear-changes. When the manual was introduced, Ian Hoban said:

With the manual transmission option for the V6 F-types, we've gone to intricate lengths to engineer a very precise, technical and responsive level of interaction between the driver, the

For some enthusiasts the introduction of a manual gearbox option finally made the F-type into a true sports car.
JAGUAR

clutch and the transmission shift mechanism. It's one for the driving purists – and I count myself as one of them.

A change enthusiasts would have been more wary of was the switch from hydraulic assistance for the steering to electro-mechanical assistance. The move had been driven by the aim

of reducing fuel consumption and CO_2 emissions – hydraulic assistance robs power from the engine all the time, whereas electric assistance only uses power when it's actually doing work.

It was a move that most car manufacturers were making, but at some cost: electric power assist earned an early

An F-type V8 R Convertible replaced the V8 S and was available in two- or four-wheel drive.
JAGUAR

reputation for feeling artificial and lacking the kind of feedback that was essential for an enthusiastic driver. Jaguar said its engineers had spent five years perfecting the electric assistance, and that it was now confident that it could provide the response and feel expected in an F-type, which was the first Jaguar to have the system fitted.

The package of revisions for the 2016 model year also included a new instrument cluster, a faster infotainment system with geographical data stored on an SD card, and two new services that connected to the user's smartphone. InControl Secure alerted the driver if the car was stolen, and InControl Remote could check vehicle information such as whether the car was locked and the level of fuel in the tank,

and could start the engine or set the climate-control system to a specific temperature.

There was also a Sport Design exterior styling pack with a new splitter, sills, venturi and (for the coupé only) a fixed rear wing. In addition there was now the option of a carbonfibre coupé roof, which, at 4.25kg (9.4lb), was even lighter than the aluminium pressing it replaced. It reduced the overall weight, lowered the centre of gravity and – probably most importantly – looked great. Torque vectoring by braking, previously only available on the F-type R coupé, could now be specified across the whole range. The range was now a little different, too, as there was a new F-type R convertible replacing the V8 S convertible, and available with either rear- or four-wheel drive.

Manual and AWD F-types were revealed at the Los Angeles show in November 2014.

JAGUAR

BLOODHOUND'S FAST RESPONSE F-TYPE

Jaguar announced in 2014 that it was supporting Bloodhound, a World Land Speed Record project aiming to be the first to achieve 1,000mph (1,600km/h) on land. A four-wheel-drive F-type R coupé rapid response vehicle was unveiled at the Coventry Motofest event the following year.

The F-type had already carried out a successful test of communications equipment, racing across the Hakskeen Pan in South Africa while a jet aircraft flew towards it at 500mph (800km/h) just 50ft (15m) off the ground while testing the communications, which will be used between the project base and driver Andy Green in Bloodhound SSC.

In June 2015 Green drove an F-type R coupé at over 180mph (290km/h) on a former military runway at Bentwaters in Suffolk to test Bloodhound SSC's parachute braking system. The F-type had a modified rear window and structural supports for Bloodhound's teardrop-shaped parachute cans. Green released the parachute using a cockpit button, subjecting the F-type to a drag force equivalent to one tonne. The F-type was also used to validate the design of a drogue chute, which inflates and pulls out the main chute.

Sadly the Bloodhound SSC project went into administration in October 2018, but the car and the intellectual property associated with it did find a buyer, and the project is now back on track.

Andy Green with Bloodhound SSC and F-type R AWD, which will be used as a rapid response vehicle.
JAGUAR

An F-type R AWD carried out a successful parachute deployment test for Bloodhound SSC in 2015.
JAGUAR

TEAM SKY F-TYPE S20C

One of the first projects from JLR's Special Vehicle Operations was to design, engineer and build a bespoke F-type coupé support vehicle for the Team Sky cycle racing operation. Jaguar was an official supplier to the team from its inception in 2010. More usually the team used Jaguar XF Sportbrakes and later F-Paces as their support vehicles.

Known as the S20C, the F-type was to be used during Stage 20 of the 2014 Tour de France, between Bergerac and Périgueux. It was based on a left-hand-drive F-type R V8 coupé, bearing the registration JF14SKY, and was finished in Team Sky's usual black and cyan livery both inside and out. The rear window was replaced by a bespoke carbonfibre panel to locate the rear wheels of two Pinarello Bolide TT bikes, plus another pair of spare wheels. The front wheel of each bike nestled into a carbonfibre channel added on top of the F-type's roof.

The bikes were securely fastened to the car with a bespoke aluminium alloy quick-release clamp, which had been tested at over 100mph (160km/h). Cargo netting was installed inside, and there was a separate electric supply in the boot to provide power for the radios, amplifiers, microphones, horns and monitors necessary for communications between Team Sky's sports director and the riders.

F-type S20C was a one-off built for the Team Sky cycling outfit.
JAGUAR

Two Pinarello time-trial bikes could be carried in a bespoke mounting on the back of the S20C.
JAGUAR

ABOVE: **The bike rack was a new carbonfibre moulding that replaced the rear screen.**
JAGUAR

LEFT: **A bespoke bracket retained the bikes at over at 100mph (160km/h).**
JAGUAR

S20C was finished in Team Sky's black and cyan colours inside and out.
JAGUAR

continued overleaf

TEAM SKY F-TYPE S20C *continued*

ABOVE LEFT: **Radios and other communications equipment were installed.**
JAGUAR

ABOVE RIGHT: **Team Sky's Sir Dave Brailsford, Richie Porte and Geraint Thomas with the S20C.**
JAGUAR

**The Team Sky
F-type is now
on display in
Jaguar Heritage's
Collections Centre
at Gaydon.**
AUTHOR

THE BRITISH DESIGN EDITION

The spring of 2016 brought good news for F-type convertible buyers, as the boot was reshaped to provide a welcome eight extra litres of storage, augmenting the rather meagre luggage space that had been widely criticised when the car was launched.

There was also a new model, the British Design Edition, based on the V6 S coupé and convertible with manual or automatic transmission and rear- or four-wheel drive. It was available in four colours, each one inspired by the colour palette of the Union Jack – Caldera Red, Glacier White, Ultra Blue and Ultimate Black. It had 20in Cyclone alloy wheels with a unique satin-grey finish, shod with vast 255/35R20 tyres at the front and 295/30R20s at the rear. Inside them was the Super Performance brake system with 380mm

front discs, 376mm rear discs, and red calipers (black was an option).

The Sport Design pack was standard, including a gloss black front splitter, body-coloured sill extensions and a body-coloured rear venture, plus a fixed rear wing on the coupé. The interior had Jet (black) premium leather with contrast stitching in red, ivory or Reims Blue, and carbonfibre trim on the centre console instead of the aluminium trim of the standard V6 S. The console, headrests and sill protectors all had special badging.

The British Design Edition had upgraded stereo equipment with a 380W Meridian ten-speaker system, or a twelve-speaker 770W system, where the InControl Touch Plus infotainment system was specified. The infotainment system's InControl Remote app was now available for the Apple Watch, so drivers could lock and unlock the F-type, check the fuel level, find the car on a map, and even pre-set the climate control or start the engine – all from the smart watch.

The British Design Edition of 2016 was available in four colours, inspired by the Union Jack.
JAGUAR

British Design Edition cars had a unique look with bigger wheels and brakes, gloss-black exterior elements, and special Union Jack-themed badges.
JAGUAR

The 20in Cyclone wheels were finished in satin black. The Super Performance brakes had bigger discs and red or black calipers.

JAGUAR

The British Design Edition interior was in black leather with contrast stitching in a choice of three colours.

JAGUAR

The centre console had carbon instead of aluminium trim, and British Design Edition badging.

JAGUAR

More special badging appeared on the seat headrests.

JAGUAR

FASTER STILL: PROJECT 7, SVR AND MODIFIED F-TYPES

Jaguar unveiled a concept for a lighter, faster, more hardcore F-type at the Goodwood Festival of Speed in 2013. It would be the first of a string of faster F-types, some of them created in-house by Jaguar and some by outside companies. Most retained the basic silhouette of the standard car and concentrated on engine and suspension upgrades coupled with relatively minor cosmetic changes, but this first iteration was much more radical.

The original idea was created by Jaguar designer César Pieri. Born in Brazil to Italian parents, Pieri studied industrial design at Sao Paulo State University, then went to Milan Polytechnic to do a Master's degree in transportation and automotive design. He worked for Fiat and the Chinese/Israeli brand Qoros, and as a freelance automotive designer,

before joining Jaguar's design team as creative design manager in 2012.

Pieri was inspired by the 1950s Jaguar D-type, and came up with a concept for an F-type that paid homage to its famous forebear. He took it to design director Ian Callum, who said when the car was revealed:

When I saw this sketch of a low-screen, single-seat F-type, I felt enthused by it and wanted to take it further. As designers, our very purpose is to disrupt – to turn the norm on its head and see if it still works – and here at Jaguar, we love to push the boundaries. As a team our challenge was to take this gem of an idea, work within the limitations of production feasibility, and create something worthwhile.

Project 7 was a concept car with the emphasis on driving pleasure.
JAGUAR

Callum encouraged Pieri and Jaguar chief designer Alister Whelan to take the idea to the next stage and develop a workable concept, and Project 7 was born.

The name was a reference to Jaguar's seven victories in the Le Mans 24-hour race (with the C-type in 1951 and 1953, the D-type in 1955, 1956 and 1957, the XJR-9 in 1988 and the XJR-12 in 1990). The most radical change Pieri proposed to the exterior of the drophead F-type was the addition of a fairing behind the driver's head, reminiscent of that on the D-type and covering a roll hoop. But that was just the start of the changes to the standard F-type specification.

Because of the new rear deck the hood had to be removed, along with the electric motors that powered it, and that made a weight saving of 20kg (44lb). A shorter windscreen was fitted, and there were no side windows. At the front there was a new carbonfibre valance with a splitter that was 15cm (6in) longer, and there were carbonfibre extensions to the sills. To balance out the aero a rear wing with a 14-degree angle of attack was added, and there was a new carbonfibre diffuser to accelerate the underbody airflow and help kill lift.

The mirrors were replaced with narrower items similar to those first seen on the C-X75 concept supercar. The electric-blue paintwork with a white stripe over the nose was a modern interpretation of the livery worn by the C-types and D-types of the Scottish Écurie Écosse team, responsible for two of Jaguar's Le Mans wins.

Inside Project 7 the passenger seat was replaced by a storage unit for a custom race helmet, which was given the same blue and white livery as the car. The driver sat in a composite race seat that was trimmed in quilted leather, mounted 30mm (1.2in) lower than standard, and equipped with a four-point racing harness. The door trims were also covered in quilted leather, and there were carbonfibre inserts on the console and gear lever. Machined aluminium gearchange paddles were provided behind the steering wheel.

Power came from Jaguar's supercharged V8 engine in its most powerful 543bhp XKR-S specification, up 54bhp on the hottest production F-type available at the time, the V8 S. A free-flow exhaust was fitted, and there was a heat-resistant ceramic coating on the tailpipes to avoid heat damage to the bodywork. Power was delivered to the rear wheels only through the F-type's usual eight-speed ZF Quickshift automatic transmission and an electronic active differential. Project 7 rode 10mm (0.4in) lower than a regular F-type, but the spring rates were actually marginally softer than standard to compensate for the reduction in the car's weight. Project 7 sat on 20in Blade forged-alloy wheels with carbonfibre inserts, wrapped in Pirelli PZero tyres, 255/30s at the front and 295/30s at the back.

According to chassis engineer Mike Cross, the aims in developing the F-type production car's handling had been agility, immediate response and a 'connected' feel, which Pro-

The fairing on the rear deck of Project 7 was a homage to the 1950s D-type.
JAGUAR

Jaguar took Project 7 to the Shelsley Walsh hillclimb for its initial publicity pictures. JAGUAR

The Project 7 prototype had just one seat, plus storage for a crash helmet. JAGUAR

ject 7 built on: 'Having achieved that for the road, Project 7 has given us a unique opportunity to go that little bit further. It's visceral in every sense – its response, its sound and its sheer performance. I'm very much looking forward to driving it at Goodwood.'

After driving the concept car for *Top Gear* magazine, Dan Read decided that it was less friendly than the regular F-type V8, and was 'a car that's easier to unsettle, but also one that's less likely to help you out once you've busted the limit of grip'.

PROJECT 7 IN PRODUCTION

The Project 7 concept generated considerable interest when Cross drove it up the Goodwood hill during the Festival of Speed. A year later, on the eve of the 2014 Festival of Speed, Jaguar made the official announcement that Project 7 would go into very limited production. Just 250 examples would be built at Jaguar Land Rover's new Special Vehicle Operations facility in Ryton. It was Jaguar's fastest production car since the XJ220, and at the time the most powerful road car it had ever offered.

Project 7 was the most extreme F-type yet.
JAGUAR

The Project 7 production car made its dynamic debut at the Le Mans Classic in 2014, alongside examples of the car that inspired it – the Le Mans-winning D-type.
JAGUAR

Production Project 7 was significantly improved compared to the concept car of a year earlier.
JAGUAR

The adjustable rear wing and driver fairing made Project 7 easy to identify.
JAGUAR

BELOW: **Carbon ceramic brakes were standard.**
JAGUAR

A few changes were made to Project 7 to turn it into a production car, notably abandoning the single-seater layout of the concept to make the production car a more practical two-seater. Carbon ceramic matrix brakes, an option on the F-type R, were fitted as standard, with 398mm discs and six-piston calipers at the front and 380mm rear discs with four-piston calipers. Project 7 also had the torque vectoring by braking system as standard to sharpen its handling.

SVO redeveloped the F-type's suspension for Project 7, with new front knuckles, which increased negative camber on the front wheels from 0.5 to 1.5 degrees to give the front end more bite. Continental ForceContact tyres were standard. There were also new suspension top mounts at the front and revised anti-roll bars front and rear. Height-adjustable spring/damper units were fitted all round, and there was a re-think on the spring rates, which were increased by a massive 80 per cent at the front and 8 per cent at the rear.

The Adaptive Dynamics adaptive damping system and stability control systems were recalibrated to suit the Project 7. A Dynamic Mode, selectable using the dashboard touchscreen, firmed up the suspension damping, reduced the amount of steering assistance, sharpened the throttle response and speeded up gearchanges.

A new control map for the engine management system boosted the V8 to 567bhp, up 25bhp on the concept, giving the Project 7 production car 0–60mph acceleration in 3.8sec, with the top speed limited to the same 186mph (300km/h) as other V8 F-types.

While the mechanicals had been subject to further development for the production car, the shape remained close to the no-compromise silhouette of the concept. The windscreen was 114mm (4.5in) shorter than on the F-type Convertible, reducing the overall height of the car by

30.5mm (1.2in), and for the production car there were new side windows to match the lower profile. A 'Bimini' roof clipped to the header rail to offer rudimentary weather protection; when not in use it could be folded and stowed in the 196ltr (7cu ft) boot. The combination of the bigger front splitter and (now adjustable) rear wing developed 177 per cent more downforce than previous F-types. The

production car was 45kg (99lb) lighter than the F-type convertible but about 35kg (77kg) heavier than the concept had been due to the addition of the hood, side windows and passenger seat.

As standard, the Project 7 was fitted with conventional seatbelts that were easier to live with than the race harness fitted to the concept car, but buyers who wanted the

The Project 7 production car had two seats rather than one.
JAGUAR

The extended front splitter helped to cut lift significantly.
JAGUAR

**Jaguar design
director Ian Callum
with the production
Project 7 at
Goodwood.**
JAGUAR

Jaguar F-Type Project 7 (2014)

Chassis and body

Type	Aluminium monocoque chassis/body; two-door two-seat roadster

Engine

Location	Front engine, longitudinal
Block material	Aluminium alloy
Head material	Aluminium alloy
Cylinders	V8
Cooling	Water
Lubrication	Wet sump
Bore × stroke	92.5 × 93.0mm
Capacity	5000cc
Main bearings	Five
Valves/operation	4 valves per cylinder, twin chain-driven overhead camshafts per cylinder bank
Compression ratio	9.5:1
Fuel system	Fuel injection
Induction system	Supercharged
Maximum power	567bhp at 6,500rpm
Maximum torque	502lb/ft (680Nm) at 2,500–5,500rpm
Transmission	Rear-wheel drive; Quickshift eight-speed automatic transmission

Suspension and steering

Front	Double wishbones, coil springs, telescopic dampers and anti-roll bar
Rear	Double wishbones, coil springs, telescopic dampers and anti-roll bar
Steering	Rack and pinion
Brakes	Front: CCM discs
	Rear: CCM discs
	Servo assisted

Dimensions

Length	4,519mm (178in)
Width	1,923mm (75.7in)
Height	1,277mm (50.3in)
Wheelbase	2,622mm (103.2in)
Unladen weight	1,585kg (3,495lb)

Performance

Top speed	186mph (300km/h)
Acceleration	0–60mph: 3.8sec

complete race-car experience could have full harnesses as an option. A steering wheel wrapped in race-style Alcantara was fitted as standard, but if the buyer preferred leather, that was available as an option. Each car would be fitted with a numbered plaque, signed by Ian Callum, located between the seats. There were five colour schemes available: Ultra Blue, Caldera Red and British Racing Green, each with white stripes, or Ultimate Black and Glacier White with grey stripes.

After its static debut in production form at the Goodwood Festival of Speed in the summer of 2014, Project 7 was seen in action for the first time at the Le Mans Classic event, where the D-type was celebrating its sixtieth anniversary. Project 7 was available for sale in the EU, South Africa, Australia, the Middle East and North Africa, Russia, Brazil, Asia Pacific and North America regions. The 250 production cars were quickly sold, and there were a rumoured 300 frustrated potential buyers on a waiting list, hoping for some of the first 250 to cancel their orders. Despite Project 7's limited weather equipment, there were eighty buyers in the UK, each of them paying £135,000 for the privilege of owning one of the most distinctive, and rare, F-types of all. Deliveries began in the middle of 2015.

One celebrity owner was AC/DC frontman Brian Johnson, who talked about his Project 7 in February 2016:

I love it. It's a proper supercar, and boy oh boy, does it have some grunt to it! While it's blisteringly fast, I feel so safe in it. I love the steering, the handling, and those carbon ceramic brakes are amazing. The discs are as big as the wheels on my racing Mini. Just listen to that noise from the exhaust: who needs a stereo when you have a soundtrack like this?

The Project 7 lived at Johnson's Florida home and was driven at least twice a week:

'These are living things that need to be exercised. My favourite drive with the Project 7 is my local State Road 64 from Bradenton over towards Sebring. It's full of bends, elevation changes and lovely long straights. You can really open it up.'

PROJECT 7 IN THE PRESS

Tom Ford drove the Project 7 production car for *Top Gear*, and wondered whether a duck-tail spoiler would have looked better than the big adjustable wing. Overall he decided that the styling of the Project 7 'catches your eye in all the best ways, without being pastiche'. To Ford's surprise, the Project 7 proved to be a good cruiser over 700 test miles (1,100km) on UK roads, though inevitably the cabin with its lower screen and side windows was windier than an F-type convertible. Ford explained that the Project 7 was 'not subtle, but it is joyously characterful, and a little bit addictive'.

He praised the refinement of the V8 engine, the seamless gear shifting and the strong brakes, but disliked the steering, which was 'way too light at speed'. The Jaguar had good balance, he said, but had enough power to swap ends easily when provoked. Ford said the Project 7 was 'too heavy and hot-rod' to be a competitor to a Porsche 911 GT3, but instead offered plenty of character and driver appeal.

Ben Barry in *CAR* said the lower windscreen and side windows gave the cabin a more open feel, but driver and passenger could still hold a conversation at speed, and even tall drivers could see below the windscreen header. Barry said the V8 offered 'one of the best soundtracks you can treat your lugs to', and there was plenty of performance, coupled to a chassis that made the Project 7 'an inherently well-balanced, playful car' and (in contrast what *Top Gear* had felt about the concept, with its less well-developed suspension) 'keener to self-straighten in a slide than the R'. Barry said the Dynamic Mode was best reserved for open roads or the track, where the stiffer damping, faster shifts and weightier steering all gelled.

Jethro Bovingdon also praised the Project 7's handling, writing for *Auto Express* that it offered 'greater connection with the surface, incredible turn-in accuracy but still with poise and innate balance'. Bovingdon had expected a more raw-edged car, but said the Project 7 still felt as much a GT as a sports car. It had more agility, cornering grip and traction than the standard F-type, and was great fun to drive on a circuit – despite its considerable weight and steering, which Bovingdon, like Ford, considered too light. Though he felt it could not compete dynamically with a Porsche 911 Turbo, it did offer an impressive blend of 'rarity, styling and charisma'.

Autocar's Steve Cropley noted a significant difference at speed between the relative calm of the driving seat and the blustery passenger side of the cabin, resulting from the fairing behind the driver's head smoothing the airflow. Cropley said it was possible to feel the substantially stiffer front suspension 'within your first 100 yards', and expected the Project 7 to be 'pretty damned uncomfortable' on bumpy UK roads. The best feature of the Project 7 was its combination of stability, agility and grip when braking and turning into medium-speed bends.

SPECIAL VEHICLE OPERATIONS

Special Vehicle Operations brought together a range of specialist and bespoke vehicle teams from both Jaguar and Land Rover under one roof for the first time. A £20 million, 20,000sq m headquarters building was built for SVO in 2015 on part of the site previously occupied by PSA Peugeot Citroën at Ryton in Coventry, not far from the Jaguar Land Rover headquarters and technical centre at Whitley. The new SVO facility incorporated a technical centre modelled on Formula 1 practice, a specialist manufacturing area, a dedicated paint shop, and a commissioning suite where VIP clients could discuss and decide the specification of their vehicle. SVO's remit was to develop special versions of JLR vehicles that aimed for ultimate luxury, ultimate performance or ultimate off-road ability.

The first SVO car was the Range Rover Sport SVR. Since then SVO has built the F-type Project 7 production car and F-type SVR, together with the Range Rover SV Autobiography and armoured Sentinel, and it was due to build the Range Rover SV Coupé before the project was cancelled. Jaguar Land Rover Classic has been established next door to look after the lightweight E-type and XKSS recreations and the 'reborn' Series 1 Land Rovers. SVO also produces one-off vehicles for well-heeled clients who have special requirements, and builds Jaguars and Land Rovers for special purposes, such as stunt vehicles for James Bond films, and the Sky Team Tour de France F-type.

SVO'S ALL-WEATHER F-TYPE

In 2016 JLR's Special Vehicle Operations brought together two strands of F-type development in one car. On one side there was the all-wheel-drive transmission that had been introduced in AWD models (*see* Chapter 7), while on the other, there was the more powerful engine and some of the aerodynamic refinements that had been developed for the Project 7. They came together in the F-type SVR.

When the car was unveiled, SVO managing director John Edwards explained the reasoning behind its creation:

Our objective was to take everything that our customers love about F-type – the performance, the handling, the sound, the design – and take it to a whole new level. It's a 200mph all-weather supercar. With 575PS, less weight, an uprated chassis and bespoke calibrations for the transmission and all-wheel-drive system, performance is even more accessible and exploitable. This is a car that SVO has developed for true enthusiasts, but it's one that can be enjoyed every day.

The car was based around the latest evolution of Jaguar Land Rover's 5.0-litre supercharged AJ133 V8 engine. The headline power figure of 575PS or 567bhp was the same as it had been in the Project 7, but there had been further refinement of the engine mapping, which boosted torque in the mid-range, taking the peak to 516lb/ft (700Nm), delivered in a wide range between 3,500 and 5,000rpm.

A new exhaust system made from titanium and Inconel – a nickel-chrome alloy – was capable of withstanding higher temperatures, and that meant the wall thickness could be halved to just 0.6mm. The result of this detail engineering effort was a 16kg (35lb) weight saving, and at the same time the system reduced back pressure. It also gave the SVR a

The F-type SVR married the four-wheel-drive AWD transmission to the more powerful engine of Project 7.

JAGUAR

distinctive rasping exhaust note. As on other F-types, the system incorporated active valves in the rear silencers, which opened at high engine speeds to reduce back pressure, and on the SVR the titanium valves opened earlier to let the V8 breathe better and to give the car a more purposeful bark. The system terminated in four round tailpipes, which had discreet SVR branding.

Power was delivered through the usual F-type eight-speed Quickshift automatic transmission, which was recalibrated for the SVR. The all-wheel-drive system's Intelligent Driveline Dynamics (IDD) control system was also reworked to improve the immediacy of its response and its launch behaviour under the motive force of the more powerful engine. There were also detail changes to the electronic active differential in the rear axle, and to the dynamic stability control system.

Despite the extra power and significantly improved performance potential, Jaguar said the SVR's fuel consumption and CO_2 figures on the European combined cycle were unchanged from the F-type R at 25mpg (11ltr/100km) and 269g/km. The coupé was capable of 200mph (322km/h), while the convertible could manage 'only' 195mph (314km/h), and Jaguar claimed a 0–60mph acceleration time of 3.5sec for both versions – a few tenths quicker than the already rapid Project 7, and half a second swifter than F-type R.

The SVR's suspension was revised, with a stiffer rear anti-roll bar than the F-type R but a softer front bar, together with new settings for the torque vectoring by braking system – both changes aiming to reduce understeer. The Adaptive Dynamics variable damping system was given recalibrated control software and a new specification of valving to improve high-speed control while also aiding low-speed comfort. At the rear, a new die-cast aluminium knuckle reduced camber change by 37 per cent and toe change by 41 per cent, improving stability and precision by keeping the tyres at the right attitude to the road surface. The control software for the electronic power-steering system was also revised to improve feedback.

Massive 380mm front and 376mm rear steel discs handled the braking duties, and as an option the SVR could be specified with the carbon ceramic matrix discs that had been standard on the Project 7 and optional on the F-type R. With big Monobloc calipers, and a pre-fill system that pre-emptively raised the pressure in the brake system slightly when the driver's foot came off the accelerator pedal, the carbon ceramic braking system could deliver consistent brake-pedal feel and excellent retardation even in continual use.

The brakes used huge discs: 380mm front and 376mm rear.
JAGUAR

Yellow calipers signified optional carbon ceramic brakes.
JAGUAR

The SVR ran on tyres that were 10mm wider front and rear than even the massive rubber on the F-type R, with 265-section front tyres on 9in rims and 305-section rears on 11in rims. The wheels were forged alloy, and delivered a weight saving of up to 13.8kg (30lb) per set, while the open-spoke design improved air flow to help with brake cooling. Coriolis design wheels in grey or black were the usual wear, but SVRs with carbon ceramic brakes were fitted with satin-black Maelstrom wheels as standard.

F-TYPE SVR DESIGN

The SVR's exterior appearance reflected SVO's desire to further refine the aerodynamic performance of the car. Minimizing drag to maximize performance was one important consideration, but there were others. It was also important to reduce lift to ensure the car remained stable at the very high speeds it was capable of. Another aerodynamic consideration was to ensure that enough air was available for cooling the more powerful engine, and to manage the expulsion of hot air from the engine bay.

The SVR's front bumper was widened so that it shrouded the front wheels more effectively, reducing drag by encouraging the air flow around the tyres and helping to keep it attached to the sides of the car. Apertures in the front wheel-arch liners, which relieved the build-up of high pressure air through the vents in the wings, reduced drag and front-end lift.

The front valance and undertray contributed to improved cooling for the more powerful engine, aided by new louvre-design bonnet vents. An undertray beneath the rear suspension helped to accelerate the airflow under the rear axle, reducing the pressure of the air and sucking the back of the car towards the road to counteract lift generated by the body at speed. The revised exhaust system had two side-mounted silencers and this allowed the incorporation of a venturi in the middle which helped to accelerate the air under the car and further aid lift reduction.

But the most effective lift-reducing device on the SVR was its deployable carbonfibre rear wing. In the lowered position the SVR's wing helped to improve drag by 7.5 per cent, and reduced lift by a spectacular 45 per cent, compared to the

The front bumper was wider to push air around the bigger tyres, reducing drag.

JAGUAR

Louvre-design bonnet vents helped to cool the more powerful engine.
JAGUAR

The carbonfibre rear wing contributed to significant decreases in lift and drag.
JAGUAR

Wing vents released high-pressure air from the wheel wells.
JAGUAR

The SVR's Inconel exhaust was lighter and reduced back pressure. The four tailpipes had SVR branding.
JAGUAR

F-type R in the same situation. The wing raised automatically at 60mph (97km/h) on the convertible or 70mph (113km/h) on the coupé when in Normal mode, or at any speed when Dynamic mode was selected. In this position the wing contributed to a 2.5 per cent reduction in drag and a 15 per cent reduction in lift compared to the F-type R with its rear spoiler deployed. The new wing meant the SVR had less drag and less lift both in the lower default position and the higher 'deployed' position than the mainstream F-types. The wing was a delete option for those who wanted their SVR to be a little more subtle, but without it SVO limited the top speed to the same 186mph (300km/h) as the regular F-type R.

The F-type SVR tipped the scales at 25kg (55lb) lighter than the F-type R AWD, and for further weight savings there were the options of a carbonfibre roof panel and a carbon

The **SVR** interior added suede-cloth trim and quilted leather. **Black was standard, but this is the Siena tan option.**
JAGUAR

BELOW: **SVR logos on the seats, dashboard and steering wheel left you in no doubt about what you were driving.**
JAGUAR

pack comprising the front chin section, bonnet louvres, wing vent trims and door mirror caps. Specifying the carbon panels together with carbon ceramic brakes saved a further 25kg (55lb).

The SVR's interior was given fourteen-way adjustable SVR performance seats with a 'lozenge quilt' pattern, contrast stitching, micro-piping and headrests with embossed SVR logos. Black leather was standard, with a black suede-cloth covering for the instrument cluster and the centre console. Siena Tan and red leather were also available, and when these were specified, the instrument panel received a full leather cover. As standard the steering wheel was black leather with black painted spokes and contrast stitching in a choice of four colours. There was also the option of leather and suede-cloth trim, which gave the interior a more purposeful, race-car vibe. Behind the wheel there were new aluminium shift paddles that were larger than those in other F-type models.

The SVR received an upgraded infotainment system based around an 8in capacitive touch screen. The standard InControl Touch system included a 380W Meridian surround-sound audio system, while the optional InControl Touch

Plus system upgraded the audio to 770W. Both systems supported the latest InControl Remote functionality, which could lock and unlock the doors, check vehicle information such as the fuel level or mileage, locate the car on a map, or even start the car and set the climate-control system temperature, all using an iOS smartphone app. The system could also interface with an Apple Watch.

The **SVR** is the fastest, most powerful and most exhilarating **F-type** – for the moment.
JAGUAR

BELOW: *Fast and Furious* star Michelle Rodriguez reached an indicated 201mph (323km/h) in an F-type SVR on a closed road in Nevada in 2016.
JAGUAR

The front end of the 2018 model year SVR received a makeover, and there were improvements to the infotainment system.
JAGUAR

Jaguar F-Type SVR (2016)

Chassis and body

Type	Aluminium monocoque chassis/body; two-door two-seat coupé or convertible

Engine

Location	Front engine, longitudinal
Block material	Aluminium alloy
Head material	Aluminium alloy
Cylinders	V8
Cooling	Water
Lubrication	Wet sump
Bore × stroke	92.5 × 93.0mm
Capacity	5000cc
Main bearings	Five
Valves/operation	4 valves per cylinder, twin chain-driven overhead camshafts per cylinder bank
Compression ratio	9.5:1
Fuel system	Fuel injection
Induction system	Supercharged
Maximum power	567bhp at 6,500rpm
Maximum torque	516lb/ft (700Nm) at 3,500–5,000rpm
Transmission	Rear-wheel drive; Quickshift eight-speed automatic transmission

Suspension and steering

Front	Double wishbones, coil springs, telescopic dampers and anti-roll bar
Rear	Double wishbones, coil springs, telescopic dampers and anti-roll bar
Steering	Rack and pinion, electromechanical assistance
Brakes	Front: 380mm ventilated discs
	Rear: 376mm ventilated discs
	Servo assisted

Dimensions

Length	4,475mm (176.2in)
Width	1,923mm (75.7in)
Height	1,311mm (51.6in)
Wheelbase	2,622mm (103.2in)
Unladen weight	1,705kg (3,759lb)

Performance

Top speed	200mph (322km/h)
Acceleration	0–60mph: 3.5sec

In the UK the F-type SVR went on sale at £110,000 for the coupé or £115,485 for the convertible, both £18,000 more than the corresponding F-type R AWD models. That made the SVR the most expensive core F-type model on offer (though the limited run Project 7 was even more). Probably the closest rival for the SVR on price and performance was the Mercedes-AMG GT S at £110,510, while the similarly powerful Aston Martin V12 Vantage S was £28,000 more, and the Porsche 911 Turbo S was £35,000 more.

For the 2018 model year the SVR gained LED headlamps and rear lights, and a new front bumper. There were also new magnesium-framed seats that saved 8kg (18lb), better interior trim, and an upgraded InControl Touch Pro infotainment system with better graphics than before. Jaguar now offered a phone app that could overlay speed, revs and lateral acceleration on to GoPro videos, for the best possible coverage of track-day exploits.

SVR REACTION

Press responses to the SVR tended to praise the improvements in handling, but questioned whether SVO's F-type could be worth virtually twice as much as an entry-level model – or whether it could match up to illustrious rivals from the likes of Porsche, Mercedes, Aston Martin and others.

Dan Prosser, writing for *Evo*, said the SVR had improvements in many areas over the F-type AWD, but that its advantages were marginal. Like the standard F-type, it felt stiff at low speed, but the ride smoothed out as the speed climbed, and beyond about 40mph (64km/h) the SVR rode marginally better than more lowly F-types, despite its sporting bias. The prodigious power output made it easy to adjust the SVR's attitude out of a corner using more or less throttle, with the four-wheel-drive system quickly pulling the car back straight.

'That gives you enormous faith in the car,' Prosser wrote, 'so you can hustle it at huge speeds without ever feeling as though it might bite.' Prosser summed up the SVR's raw pace as 'staggering'. But he said the SVR offered incremental improvements over the F-type R rather than a step change, and mused on what he felt was the 'untapped sporting potential lurking within the F-type'.

CAR's Gareth Evans felt the SVR was most fun when steering inputs were kept to a minimum, which encouraged the four-wheel-drive system to direct most of the engine torque to the rear wheels and resulted in the SVR drifting out of

corners. The trick, Evans felt, was to get the power on early into corners. If the driver was prepared to learn how to get the best from it the SVR was, Evans wrote, 'devastatingly quick'. He felt the optional carbon brakes were a vital extra despite their £8,000 cost: 'Few manufacturers manage the blend of low-speed manners and high-speed braking quite so impressively.' But Evans was unimpressed by the 'cheap-feeling' gearshift paddles and the old-fashioned infotainment system.

In *Motor Sport* Andrew Frankel considered it was not the SVR's extra speed that was obvious, as its greater fluency. The SVR was, he said, better at handling the power than any previous F-type, and was also the best riding version so far. Having questioned Jaguar's ability to create a convincing performance coupé in the £100,000+ sector, Frankel was pleased that the F-type SVR was exactly what an SVO product should be: '...not simply faster, which is easy to do, but better in every way. That's far more difficult, yet has been resoundingly achieved here.'

Erin Baker in *The Daily Telegraph* said the combination of extra power and less weight was not enough, and that a wealthy car collector wanted 'a little fairy dust too: bespoke materials, a different sound system, and more'. Baker felt there should have been 'a few more points of differentiation, a feeling of belonging to a rarefied club' – but despite that said the SVR was an understated success.

Alan Taylor-Jones drove the revised 2018 model year car for *Autocar* and felt the SVR's weight worked against it on the track, and it felt more at home on the road. The improved interior was welcome, but the touchscreen infotainment system was still harder to use than systems such as BMW's iDrive, operated by a rotary controller. Ultimately *Autocar* felt that only a serious Jaguar fan would choose the F-type SVR over a 911 Turbo, Audi R8 or McLaren 540C.

BACK ON TRACK

The SVR formed the basis of two racing cars, which returned works-built Jaguars to the race track for the first time in a couple of decades in 2018. The F-type SVR GT4s, which made their debut at the Oulton Park round of the British GT Championship in March, were run by a privateer team, Invictus Games Racing. The team was the brainchild of James Holder, co-founder of the Superdry fashion brand, who competed in the GT championship himself in 2016 in an Aston Martin V8 Vantage GT4. Holder saw drivers with physical disabilities

The Invictus Games Racing team was launched at the Autosport International show in January 2018. The team races a pair of GT4-spec F-types built by Jaguar Special Vehicle Operations.

The F-type GT4 cars are based on SVR models but with rear-wheel drive and restrictors limiting power output to around 450–500bhp.
JAGUAR

racing competitively in the championship, and aimed to found a team that could get injured servicemen into racing.

The Invictus Games Foundation became a partner, and the Forces' motorsport charity Mission Motorsport carried out a driver recruitment and training programme. The four drivers chosen were Para Basil Rawlinson, RAF sergeant Ben

Norfolk, Commando Paul Vice and Marine Steve McCulley, who would be mentored by pro drivers Jason Wolfe and Matthew George. Ex-servicemen and women were also recruited to join the race team. Meanwhile Holder commissioned Jaguar Land Rover Special Vehicle Operations to design and build two GT4 cars based on the F-type SVR.

To comply with the series regulations, the SVR's four-wheel drive was replaced by rear-wheel drive, and intake air restrictors were fitted to the 5.0-litre AJ133 V8 engine, limiting power to 450–500bhp. Power was taken through an Xtrac six-speed sequential gearbox with a pneumatically operated paddle-shift gearchange system. Alcon race-spec six-piston front brake calipers clamped 380mm discs at the front, and there were four-piston calipers and 343mm discs at the rear. The suspension used Eibach springs and Bilstein racing dampers, which were adjustable for bump and rebound.

The SVR body was stripped of trim inside and out, and the side and rear glass windows were replaced with virtually unbreakable polycarbonate. Composite panels replaced the front splitter, bonnet and tailgate, while the doors had carbonfibre inner frames and aluminium outer skins. Inside the car there was a 120ltr ATL bag fuel tank, a bespoke roll cage to MSA/FIA regulations, a composite race seat and FIA-spec six-point harness, and window safety nets. The complete GT4 car weighed 1,450kg (3,197lb), which was more than 250kg (551lb) lighter than the road-going SVR.

Holder spoke at the team's launch at the Autosport International show in January 2018:

We are not under any illusions. I know personally how difficult this level of racing is, and we're a brand-new team starting out. In the first season we will primarily be competing between each of our own cars, but we will take every opportunity to finish as high up the pack as humanly possible in every race. Our shared desire and goal is ultimately to win races.

Jaguar F-Type GT4 (2018)

Chassis and body

Type	Aluminium monocoque chassis/body with composite front end and aluminium alloy doors; two-door two-seat coupé

Engine

Location	Front engine, longitudinal
Block material	Aluminium alloy
Head material	Aluminium alloy
Cylinders	V8
Cooling	Water
Lubrication	Wet sump
Bore × stroke	92.5 × 93.0mm
Capacity	5000cc
Main bearings	Five
Valves/operation	4 valves per cylinder, twin chain-driven overhead camshafts per cylinder bank
Compression ratio	9.5:1
Fuel system	Fuel injection
Induction system	Supercharged, with mandatory restrictor
Maximum power	450–500bhp
Maximum torque	n/a
Transmission	Rear-wheel drive; Xtrac six-speed sequential transmission with Shiftec pneumatic paddleshift

Suspension and steering

Front	Double wishbones, Eibach coil springs, Bilstein two-way adjustable telescopic dampers and anti-roll bar
Rear	Double wishbones, Eibach coil springs, Bilstein two-way adjustable telescopic dampers and anti-roll bar
Steering	Rack and pinion, electromechanical assistance
Brakes	Front: 380mm ventilated discs with Alcon six-piston calipers. Rear: 343mm ventilated discs with Alcon four-piston calipers. Servo assisted
Wheels	11 × 18in Rimstock aluminium alloy
Tyres	305 × 660 × 18in Pirelli racing tyres

Dimensions

Length	4,482mm (176.5in)
Width	1,923mm (75.7in)
Height	1,314mm (51.7in)
Wheelbase	2,622mm (103.2in)
Unladen weight	1,450kg (3,197lb)

Performance

Top speed	n/a
Acceleration	n/a

This dream won't happen overnight, but during the journey I can promise fans that we will have inspirational drivers, great stories, innovative technology, and the coolest looking and sounding cars on the circuit.

Both F-types finished the two Oulton races, giving the team a solid start, and for the rest of the season the F-types generally made it to the flag, though they struggled to match the pace of the GT4 competition. The team appeared at the Goodwood Festival of Speed in 2018, taking part in 'Q&A' sessions on the Jaguar Land Rover stand to explain what the team was about, and before the Silverstone round of the championship in June the team held its own event for the Invictus Games UK community. Before the final round of the championship, at Donington in September, Prince Harry met with the drivers, their families and team engineers before starting up car 44.

Before the 2019 season the cars were rebuilt by David Appleby Engineering, and the team's performance improved significantly in its second year. At Oulton Park, McCulley shared the single F-type GT4 entry with George, and the pair claimed first and second in class, plus third overall in the second race. Vice and George finished on the podium at Snetterton, McCulley and George recorded a similar result at Spa, and then at the last round at Donington, McCulley and Vice shared the car in what Vice said was sure to be 'the quickest "all disabled" driver pairing on the whole grid'.

VIP PREDATOR

Design and tuning company VIP Design unveiled what it claimed was the world's most powerful F-type in April 2016. The company, a collaboration between tuning operation Paramount Performance and ECU remap specialists Viezu Technologies, offered tuning and styling packages for the F-type, and could boost the V8 engine to as much as 650bhp through a combination of hardware and software upgrades. VIP Design managing director Phil Busby explained the idea behind the car:

> Since the Jaguar F-Type was launched, the sleek lines and V8 engine were always going to lend themselves to power upgrades, and appeal to passionate drivers who are never going to settle for stock options. Our new package has created the most exciting F-Type available in the world and is certain to thrill serious petrol-heads anywhere.

The engine improvements began with high-flow air filters to improve throttle response, and a smaller pulley for the supercharger to increase its speed. An ECU remap, which took the team three weeks to develop on a dyno, raised boost pressure and increased fuelling to match, and was said to improve power across the whole rev range. VIP Design also fitted a high-performance exhaust system, Busby explained:

The VIP Predator offered 650bhp and a package of styling tweaks.
VIP DESIGN

NÜRBURGRING TAXI

The F-type SVR was one of the cars involved in Jaguar's Co-Pilot Nordschleife and Race Taxi services around the famous Nürburgring Nordschleife circuit in Germany. The latest programme, Jaguar Race Taxi, ran between May and November 2018. For €199 passengers could book a lap of the 12.9-mile 'Green Hell' alongside a professional driver in the F-type SVR or an XJR575, and would receive a DVD with an in-car video of their lap. The cars were fitted with Recaro race seats and roll cages.

'A ride in the F-type SVR and XJR575 Race Taxi is a thrilling and truly unforgettable experience for any car enthusiast – or anybody who just enjoys going very fast!' said Phil Talboys, Jaguar Land Rover's European engineering operations manager. 'Our highly experienced professional drivers are veterans of the Nürburgring 24-hour race, making them uniquely qualified to show customers the true potential of these extraordinary supercharged V8 Jaguars.'

Jaguar's Race Taxi service offered Nürburgring laps in the F-type SVR and the XJR575.
JAGUAR

The exhaust wasn't deep enough – more of a shriek than a V8 rumble. The full manifold back high performance exhaust system is switchable, allowing different purr levels – loud and really loud! You can't help but grin every time you press the button.

Suspension upgrades included a 30mm (1.2in) drop in ride height, and stiffer bushes were said to improve poise and

responsiveness, 'transforming the handling of the standard F-type'. There was also a package of styling changes, with bonnet vents, front and rear splitters (said to be 'adding downforce and style') and a rear diffuser, all in polished carbonfibre. Buyers could choose from twenty-four aluminium alloy wheel designs, and twenty-eight body colours.

VIP Design fitted the package at its studio in Warwickshire, with prices starting from £12,600. Later, 600bhp and

670bhp versions were introduced, and VIP Design also released upgrade packages for the V6 engine – taking it to 440bhp, or even 480bhp.

LISTER'S 666BHP F-TYPE

In 2016 there was another contender for the title of 'most powerful F-type'. Brian Lister built Jaguar-engined racing cars back in the days of the C-type and D-type, famously campaigned by the Scottish driver Archie Scott Brown. The brand was revived in the 1980s by Laurence Pearce, who built tuned XJ-Ss followed by the 7.0-litre Jaguar V12-engined Lister Storm. Andrew and Lawrence Whittaker took over in 2013, and the company has since revived its 1950s models and set about tuning modern Jaguars.

Lister's take on the F-type was unveiled at the Historic Motorsport International show in February 2018 under the name Thunder. Lister claimed 666bhp at 6,000rpm and peak torque of 720lb/ft, derived using custom supercharger

Lister raced Jaguar-engined cars in the 1950s and 1960s. This is a Costin-bodied Lister prepared by JD Classics and driven in the Goodwood Revival Sussex Trophy by Chris Ward.
JD CLASSICS

Lister's Jaguar-engined Storm in GTL Le Mans guise in 1997.
LISTER

Lawrence Whittaker became Lister MD in 2013.
LISTER

Lister announced the F-type-based Thunder prototype early in 2018.
LISTER

Lister Thunder offered 666bhp and a 208mph (335km/h) top speed.
LISTER

pulleys and intercoolers, a new engine-management system and a new Novitec exhaust. The top speed was said to be 208mph (335km/h), 0–62mph acceleration took just over 3.0sec, and 0–100mph 6.8sec – making the new car the fastest and the most powerful that Lister had ever built. A new carbonfibre front bumper/splitter and rear bumper gave the Lister an individual appearance, and there were Lister bonnet vents and a green and yellow Lister grille badge.

There were stiffer KW springs with adjustable spring platforms so the ride height could be easily tweaked, but the dampers were standard, and there were fifteen-spoked 21in Vesson wheels sporting twenty-five section rubber at the rear. Just ninety-nine cars were to be built at a new facility in Milton Keynes, with a starting price of £139,950. Lawrence Whittaker said at the launch:

> Like Brabus and AMG with Mercedes and Alpina with BMW, we are hoping to become synonymous once again with tuning Jaguar vehicles, giving customers new enhanced, bespoke performance and design alternatives to Jaguar's acclaimed model programme. Although we are not directly affiliated with Jaguar Land Rover, Lister has a Jaguar tuning heritage dating back sixty-five years. I am utterly proud of what we have achieved, and the Thunder is just the beginning!

Richard Lane drove the Lister for *Autocar* and praised the 'superbly linear' delivery of the supercharged engine, which would have made the Thunder a viable tourer had it not been for the epically loud exhaust. But the car needed further work, as the tyres sometimes rubbed on the wheel-arch liners and the suspension could be caught out by rippled tarmac.

Evo's John Barker agreed, but noted that Lister was already revisiting the suspension settings. Unlike the standard F-type, the Lister had no active exhaust valves so it was 'incredibly loud at idle, under power and even on the overrun'. Barker said the Lister was possibly not as fast as it sounded, but praised the low-rev and mid-range power, and said it was 'one of those cars that is always travelling 20mph faster than you expect'.

In August 2018 Lister confirmed that the car had been renamed LFT-666 and had been subject to further development. It now had new Lister-designed carbonfibre panels replacing the front bumper, splitter and grille, and the rear diffuser, lip spoiler and wheel arches. The new parts were said to make the LFT-666 a 'lighter and stronger car that offers improved aerodynamics on both road and track'. There were also new alloy wheels – 9 × 21in at the front and 11.5 × 21in at the rear – with Michelin tyres, and Lister had reworked the suspension and made improvements to the interior, the quilted leather seats and the steering wheel. Just ninety-nine production cars were planned.

Lister also announced that the LFT-666's wheel and body enhancements would be available for standard F-types, with kit prices starting from £9,750, and that cars with Lister body enhancements but standard engines would be known as Lister LFTs, without the number denoting the engine power. To follow the LFT-666, Lister introduced a convertible LFT-C with an even more restricted production run of just ten examples. The company was also reported to be considering a version of the F-type SVR with a production run of 250 cars.

Further development turned the Thunder into the Lister LFT-666, unveiled in August 2018.
LISTER

The Lister LFT-666 had wider use of carbonfibre body panels and revised aerodynamics.
LISTER

ARDEN AJ23

Jochen Arden's company has been building modified Jaguars near Düsseldorf in western Germany since 1982. Arden built the first full convertible version of the XJ-S in 1985, followed by estate cars, a twin-turbo XJ40, lightweight XKs, and more. Arden first turned its attention to the F-type in 2014.

The Arden Jaguar AJ23 Race Cat had a range of exterior, interior and mechanical modifications. At the front a hand-crafted stainless-steel grille and additional flaps under the front valance gave the nose an individual appearance, while at the back there was a new diffuser that was said to improve high-speed downforce. Arden could supply the new panels made from carbonfibre composite for the ultimate in weight reduction. Inside there were carbonfibre, aluminium and wood trim options, plus thick pile carpets, aluminium pedals and bi-colour leather seats. A sports spring kit reduced the ride height by around 25mm (1in), and there were 21in multi-spoke alloy wheels with 30mm spacers.

German Jaguar tuner Arden turned its attention to the F-type in 2014.
ARDEN

New front and rear aerodynamic panels and a sports exhaust were central to Arden's AJ23 Race Cat.
ARDEN

Extra flaps added under the front valance could be specified in carbonfibre.
ARDEN

ABOVE LEFT: **Arden's 21in Sportline wheel was a three-piece item with five double spokes.**
ARDEN

ABOVE RIGHT: **The Arden Race Cat's exterior changes were subtle and well thought out.**
ARDEN

Race-style aluminium alloy pedals were one of Arden's most affordable modifications.
ARDEN

Interiors could be retrimmed to the customer's requirements, with bi-colour seats one option.
ARDEN

A new stainless-steel exhaust system, with sports catalysts, four polished tailpipes and active valving, was claimed to release about 25bhp from the V8 engine, and 20bhp from the V6. Arden could boost both engines by about 40bhp with simple tuning, while more extensive modifications with a new supercharger drive and forged pistons could bring the V8 up to 656bhp.

Arden's version of the F-type SVR introduced a new front grille with an illuminated logo, a substantial front valance carrying massive air intakes and turning vanes, new side skirts and a new rear bumper. Two alloy wheel designs were available – the established Arden Sportline three-piece wheel with five double spokes, and a new Sportline GT monobloc wheel with seventeen spokes, said to be 'tailored

143

Interior trim panels could be in aluminium, wood or even – as here – coloured weave carbonfibre.
ARDEN

to the design language and needs of the current Jaguar fleet'. Both wheels were 21in in diameter, 9.5in wide at the front and 11in at the rear, carrying 265/30ZR21 and 325/25ZR21 Continental tyres respectively. As before, the suspension was lowered 25–30mm (1–1.2in) using progressive springs.

Under the bonnet Arden comprehensively reworked the 5.0-litre V8 engine with forged pistons, a supercharger upgrade, and a new carbonfibre intake system. There was also a new engine-management system, and an Arden exhaust system with metal catalysts. The result, for an outlay of some-

thing in excess of €30,000, was a massive leap in power from the SVR's 567bhp to no less than 693bhp, together with a jump in peak torque from 516lb/ft to 644lb/ft.

The Arden AJ23 AVR is – so far – the most powerful F-type ever made (and there is talk of a wide-body conversion with even more power on the way). However, while powerful, bespoke F-types were being championed by a German tuning company, back at Whitley, Jaguar was already working on new F-types that would expand the range in an entirely different direction.

The AJ23 SVR had a new rear diffuser, an Arden exhaust and a lower ride height.
ARDEN

New monobloc seventeen-spoke alloys were designed specifically to complement modern Jaguars.
ARDEN

BELOW : **Arden's AJ23 SVR boasted 693bhp, and is the most powerful F-type yet built.**
ARDEN

CHAPTER SEVEN

FACELIFTS AND FOUR CYLINDERS

Jaguar announced an update to the F-type range early in 2017, which freshened up the appearance of the car, added some new technology and introduced new models. For the first time the F-type gained full LED headlights, though still incorporating the J-shaped daytime running light, which now doubled as the direction indicator. LED lamps were more efficient – more of the energy that they consumed was turned into useful light – and the beam could be adjusted in different ways to suit the driving conditions.

The lights could switch between four different modes – city, country, motorway and bad weather. City mode provided a wide-angle low beam helping the driver to see pedestrians and side roads more easily at up to 30mph (48km/h). Country mode activated automatically above 30mph, providing a longer, narrower beam, which improved visibility at a distance. At speeds over 56mph (90km/h) the motorway mode focused the beam still further ahead for long-range vision.

The bad weather mode was specifically designed to aid progress in heavy rain at up to 40mph (64km/h). To complement the new headlamps the rear lights were updated with darker lenses to accentuate the E-type-inspired shape.

Though most observers agreed there was little wrong with the F-type's shape, there were some changes, with new bumpers in simpler, bolder shapes that helped to provide greater differentiation between the different F-type models. The distinctive 'shark gill' apertures on each side of the main radiator grille, which had been present since the first F-types, had now gone and in their place were bigger, single apertures.

There was a new range of driver assistance systems, enabled by the adoption of a forward-facing stereo camera, already in use on other Jaguars. One of the most important of these new systems was autonomous emergency braking, which could apply the brakes automatically if it sensed that a

Early in 2017 the F-type was given a new look and new technology.
JAGUAR

ABOVE LEFT: **Full LED headlamps were adopted early in 2017 for the 2018 model year.**
JAGUAR

ABOVE RIGHT: **The rear lights gained darker lenses to accentuate their shape.**
JAGUAR

The shark-gill slots on each side of the radiator grille aperture gave way to bigger, bolder vents. This is the revised **V8 R.**
JAGUAR

collision was imminent – possibly avoiding a crash or at least mitigating its effects.

The stereo camera also provided data for lane departure warning and lane keep assist systems, which monitored the F-type's position relative to lane markers on the road. If the car drifted out of its lane a visual warning was flashed up on the instrument cluster, and the driver was also given a haptic warning – a gentle shake of the steering wheel to attract attention to the problem. If the driver took no action to bring the F-type back into its lane, a small amount of steering angle was applied by the lane keep system to bring the car back on line, though the level of steering torque it used was very small and could easily be overridden by the driver if the deviation in the car's course had been intentional.

Drifting out of lane is often caused by driver fatigue, and the F-type now included a driver condition monitor, which could

ABOVE: **The revised SVR models also had a bolder, cleaner front end.**
JAGUAR

The adoption of a forward-facing stereo camera enabled Jaguar to incorporate new driver assistance features such as autonomous emergency braking and lane assist.
JAGUAR

recognize patterns of driving typical of tired drivers, such as periods of little or no steering activity followed by sudden or excessive inputs. If it recognized a drowsy driver it could show multi-stage warnings in the instrument cluster, and sound an audible warning encouraging the driver to take a break.

The stereo camera was also used by a traffic sign recognition system, which looked out for speed limit signs – including temporary signs for roadworks – and displayed the cur-rent limit on the instrument panel. To improve the reliability of the information the camera data was cross-referenced with a speed limit database referenced by the car's position using GPS data from the navigation system. An adaptive speed limiter was also incorporated, which could reduce the F-type's speed to match the limit determined by the traffic sign recognition system, and then automatically accelerate when it recognized a higher limit had come into force.

New aluminium interior trim highlights were added for the 2018 model year.
JAGUAR

BELOW: **Magnesium-framed seats saved 8kg (17.5lb).**
JAGUAR

Alongside the safety-related systems there was a new semi-automated park assist system, which could steer the vehicle into a parallel parking space while the driver controlled the throttle and brakes. The system could also guide the F-type out of the space. It was a particular boon on the coupé, and on the convertible when the roof was raised and rear visibility restricted.

Inside the revised F-type there were new seats – lightweight and slimline, offering more lateral support and providing up to 50mm (2in) more legroom. The seats had frames that were pressure diecast in magnesium alloy, which saved more than 8kg (18lb) over the old chairs, and they had the option of both electric heating and cooling, using fans to direct cool air to the seat surfaces. There were two seat types: Sport, which was fitted to the F-type and the new F-type R-Dynamic; and Performance, fitted to the R, SVR and new 400 Sport. Each had the model's logo embossed into the headrest. The attractive Siena Tan leather option, previously available only on the SVR, was now offered across the range.

There was a new frameless rear-view mirror, a satin chrome finish for the engine start button and gearshift paddles, and what Jaguar called Noble Chrome finish on the door switches, air-vent bezels and steering wheel. Different aluminium finisher panels were used on the centre console,

A new Touch Pro infotainment system was introduced with an 8in capacitive touchscreen, which was said to be easier to use and had a 4G data connection to access online services such as real-time traffic data and live weather reports. The system had a 'commute mode', which could learn the driver's regular route and offer alternative directions to avoid congestion, using a combination of historical and real-time traffic information. A 'share ETA' function could send the car's destination, current location and estimated time of arrival to selected contacts by email or text message, and could automatically follow up with an update if the F-type was delayed on its journey. The navigation system could even show you where the nearest available parking spaces were when you arrived at your destination, and then direct you to them.

There was an interesting collaboration with GoPro, the action camera company, in the form of an app that Jaguar called ReRun and claimed as a world first. The app could combine real-time video from a GoPro camera mounted on the car with vehicle performance data such as speed, throttle position, gear selection, braking force and lateral g-force – ideal for recording track-day exploits, for example. The video could be downloaded to a phone and shared on social media.

depending on the model: the base-model F-type had a simple, knurled aluminium; the R-Dynamic had a finish called Delta; and the R models had a Linear Vee finish, which incorporated an etched R logo. There was also the option of a carbonfibre centre console finisher across the range.

ABOVE: **The new TouchPro infotainment system offered tablet-style operation and access to online information services.**
JAGUAR

RIGHT: **The ReRun app provided an easy way to capture and replay driving footage using a GoPro camera, overlaid with speed, gear, rpm and other data.**
JAGUAR

Once the camera was set up it could be controlled from the built-in infotainment system.
JAGUAR

Driving footage could be shared using social media and viewed on other devices.
JAGUAR

Two Meridian audio systems were available. The standard system had ten speakers, while there was an optional Surround Sound system boasting no fewer than twelve speakers. The system could display Gracenote album art, which was stored on a solid-state drive, also offering a massive 10GB of storage space for media files. A Spotify app could learn listening habits and recommend new tracks, working offline in areas with a poor internet connection to provide access to content already downloaded.

R-DYNAMIC AND 400 SPORT

To mark the revisions to the F-type, Jaguar introduced a special launch model called the 400 Sport, which it said would be available only in the 2018 model year. The 400 Sport could be ordered in rear-wheel-drive or all-wheel-drive forms, all of them with a mechanical limited-slip differential at the rear. Power came from a new 400PS (395bhp) version of the V6 engine, complemented by the Super Performance braking

The facelifted F-types were introduced with a launch model, the 400 Sport.
JAGUAR

BELOW RIGHT: **The 400 Sport had distinctive wheels and badging.**
JAGUAR

option with bigger 380mm front discs and 376mm rear discs, along with black calipers carrying '400 Sport' badges.

The unique 20in five-spoke wheels were finished in satin grey. The 400 came with the Configurable Dynamics system, which enabled personalization of the gear-shift speed, throttle response and steering weighting. There were yellow 400 Sport badges on the front and rear, contrasting with the metallic paintwork in Indus Silver, Santorini Black or Yulong White. More badges were found inside, on the steering wheel, dashboard and seats, and there was yellow contrast stitching throughout.

Alongside the short-run 400 Sport there was a new core model, the R-Dynamic, available with either the 340PS (335bhp) or 380PS (375bhp) V6 engines. The new model had distinctive 19in and 20in alloy wheel designs, and for further differentiation the bezels around the front bumper apertures were finished in gloss black, as were the front splitter, bonnet vents, sills and rear diffuser. The R-Dynamic was available with either automatic or manual gearboxes, in rear-wheel drive only for the lower-output engine, but with a choice of rear-wheel drive or four-wheel drive for the 380PS V6.

Autocar's Steve Cropley drove the 400 Sport and noted that it offered a focus on driving, with the agility of the V6-engined F-type and performance almost on a par with the V8 but for a lower price. The extra 20bhp at the top end of the rev range compared to the V6 S was barely noticeable because the automatic transmission changed up around 5,000rpm, but holding the engine to the red line

and changing manually was barely any quicker. Cropley felt that for a serious driver, 'Jaguar has got the specification of it so right.'

John McIlroy drove the new F-types for *Auto Express* and was impressed by the 400 Sport's brakes, which had a 'pleasing bite' and resisted fade even on the heavier convertible. The rest of the F-type was 'as strong as ever', with rapid performance, but still without the agility of a Porsche 911 or Boxster, and with a ride that was only barely tolerable. *Auto Express* concluded that the R-Dynamic was the better buy than the 400 Sport, and at almost £6,000 less would leave cash available for a few optional extras.

400 Sport badging continued inside, on the dashboard and steering wheel.
JAGUAR

BELOW RIGHT: Unique wheel designs in 19in and 20in sizes were available on the R-Dynamic models.
JAGUAR

ABOVE LEFT: **R-Dynamic was a new core model introduced in 2017.**
JAGUAR

R-Dynamic models featured gloss-black finish for the front bumper apertures, bonnet vents, splitter, sills and rear diffuser.
JAGUAR

Jaguar F-Type 400 Sport (2017)

Chassis and body	
Type	Aluminium monocoque chassis/body; two-door two-seat coupé or convertible

Engine	
Location	Front engine, longitudinal
Block material	Aluminium alloy
Head material	Aluminium alloy
Cylinders	V6
Cooling	Water
Lubrication	Wet sump
Bore × stroke	84.5 × 89.0mm
Capacity	2995cc
Main bearings	Five
Valves/operation	4 valves per cylinder, twin chain-driven overhead camshafts per cylinder bank
Compression ratio	10.5:1
Fuel system	150-bar fuel injection
Induction system	Supercharged
Maximum power	395bhp (400PS) at 6,500rpm
Maximum torque	339lb/ft (460Nm) at 3,500–5,500rpm
Transmission	Rear-wheel drive or four-wheel drive; Quickshift eight-speed automatic transmission

Suspension and steering	
Front	Double wishbones, coil springs, telescopic dampers and anti-roll bar
Rear	Double wishbones, coil springs, telescopic dampers and anti-roll bar
Steering	Rack and pinion, electromechanical assistance
Brakes	Front: 380mm ventilated discs
	Rear: 376mm ventilated discs
	Servo assisted

Dimensions	
Length	4,482mm (176.5in)
Width	1,923mm (75.7in)
Height	Coupé: 1,311mm (51.6in)
	Convertible: 1,308mm (51.5in)
Wheelbase	2,622mm (103.2in)
Unladen weight	Coupé: 1,594kg (3,514lb)
	Convertible: 1,614kg (3,558lb)
	Coupé AWD: 1,674kg (3,691lb)
	Convertible AWD: 1,694kg (3,735lb)

Performance	
Top speed	171mph (275km/h)
Acceleration	0–60mph: 4.8sec (AWD: 4.9sec)

CAR's Jake Groves picked up on the comfort theme, saying the ride was 'firm, but not irritatingly so', though the seats did become uncomfortable after a long motorway journey. Groves praised the 400 Sport's straight-line speed and meaty steering, which inspired confidence, but said the F-type felt 'uncomfortably wide on the road'. The engine and its spectacular sound effects were the big attraction, but the noise could sometimes be tiresome, and the price (£83,000 for *CAR*'s AWD convertible test car) was high.

INGENIUM: A NEW ENGINE FAMILY

The XK engine that powered all Jaguars from the late 1940s to the beginning of the 1970s made Jaguar synonymous with 6-cylinder engines. A V12 arrived in the 1970s, but the XK 6 remained the core engine until the 1980s, and it was replaced by another straight-six, the AJ6. It took until the 1990s for Jaguar to follow the lead of most of the US manufacturers, plus Europeans such as Mercedes, BMW and Porsche, and adopt V8 engines.

As far back as the introduction of the XK120 in 1948 Jaguar had been planning to build 4-cylinder engines, but none reached a production Jaguar until the 4-cylinder diesel version of the X-type was announced in 2002. 4-cylinder Jaguars reappeared in 2014 when Jaguar Land Rover announced the first in a new family of in-line engines, which would make their debut in the XE saloon and would subsequently end up under the bonnet of a new addition to the F-type range.

This new range of engines was called Ingenium, and was a modular family that could yield in-line 3-, 4-, 5- and 6-cylinder motors fuelled by petrol or diesel. They were

Jaguar Land Rover's modular Ingenium engine was introduced in 2015. The engines are built at the i54 facility near Wolverhampton.
JAGUAR

highly adaptable, designed to be suitable for transverse or in-line mounting, with manual or automatic transmissions and front-, rear- or four-wheel drive. Ingenium was designed to be easy to update as new technologies emerged, and was created with hybridization in mind as Jaguar Land Rover could see that future requirements would demand it.

It is almost always the case that new engines carry over something from previous generations. Jaguar's AJ6, for instance, was designed to share some of the production machinery of the V12, and the V6 engine in the F-type was based on the same block as the V8. Unusually, the powertrain engineers who created the Ingenium family were given a completely free hand to create exactly the engines that were needed. There was no need to share anything with the previous motors – in fact part of the need for the new engines

was so that JLR could get away from the Ford-built units that were a hangover from the company's ownership by the Blue Oval, and take control of its own engine supply.

Nor was there any requirement to use existing production facilities, as the Ingenium engines were to be built at JLR's brand new, £1 billion Engine Manufacturing Centre near Wolverhampton. Director of powertrain engineering Ron Lee said the clean sheet of paper approach was a major advantage:

We weren't locked into any of the usual restrictions that force engineering compromises because we had no existing production machinery that would dictate design parameters, no carryover engine architectures to utilize, and no existing factory to modify.

One of the main focuses during the design of the engines was to minimize internal friction. JLR said the Ingenium engines had up to 17 per cent less friction than the previous range, which meant that the engines wasted less of the power they produced. The reduction of friction used a variety of different technologies. The camshafts and twin balancer shafts ran in needle roller bearings rather than the more usual plain bearings, for example, and the cam drive was simplified, shortening the main drive chain and reducing the number of moving parts.

The crankshaft was offset from the centre of the block by 12mm (0.5in) to reduce the tangential forces that tended to push the pistons into the cylinder walls, increasing friction and wear. The engines were fitted with computer-controlled oil pumps and water pumps, which varied the oil and coolant flow depending on temperature, engine speed and driving conditions, reducing load on the pumps when less flow was needed and consequently reducing the power required to drive the pumps.

There were also electronically controlled piston cooling jets directing oil to the underside of the piston crowns, which could be switched off when they were not needed to speed warm-up and reduce losses. The cooling system itself was a twin circuit design that only circulated coolant through the cylinder block once the engine was warm, enabling a faster warm-up, which improved fuel economy and emissions – and also improved passenger comfort because the heater warmed the cabin more quickly.

All the Ingenium engines were turbocharged using state-of-the-art 'twin scroll' turbos to reduce lag and increase efficiency. Direct high-pressure fuel injection with an optimized spray pattern, variable valve timing and stop-start technology were also incorporated in the Ingenium design to improve overall efficiency. Jaguar Land Rover said the Ingenium was

The 300PS version of the Ingenium incorporated a twin scroll turbocharger with ceramic ball bearings to minimize friction and improve response.
JAGUAR

one of the most rigorously tested engines it had ever built, with accelerated testing equating to more than eight years of normal use. The Ingenium engines underwent 72,000 hours of running on engine dynamometers, and two million miles (three million kilometres) of road and track testing.

The first production Ingenium diesels were built at the Wolverhampton facility in 2015, and by the time petrol units came on stream in April 2017 the factory had already built more than 400,000 engines.

When the engines were launched in 2014 Jaguar Land Rover's group engineering director Dr Wolfgang Ziebart put their importance for the company into perspective:

Customers around the world are increasingly demanding cleaner running, more efficient vehicles that maintain or even enhance the performance attributes expected of a rugged all-terrain vehicle or a high-performance car. Our Ingenium engines deliver this to a new level.

Engineering and manufacturing our own engines improves our ability to react to changes in demand and improves our

ability to react to changes in legislation and competitive technologies in the future. We believe that with the range of technologies we are investing in, Jaguar Land Rover can absolutely satisfy the often conflicting requirements of delivering engaging high-performance luxury vehicles that reduce our carbon footprint in the long term.

The new engines first went into the Jaguar XE saloon in 4-cylinder diesel form offering 163PS or 180PS, and they were gradually adopted across the Jaguar Land Rover range in both diesel and petrol versions. Early reaction to JLR's new power units was broadly positive, though in some applications it was felt they could be more refined.

More powerful Ingenium engines followed: petrol versions with 200PS, 250PS and 290PS, plus a 240PS twin turbo diesel, and then in 2017 came the most powerful Ingenium yet – in fact, the most powerful 4-cylinder engine Jaguar Land Rover had ever built. It was a petrol motor with 300PS (296bhp) and 400NM of torque, and it introduced a new method of valve control that eliminated the need for a throttle.

TWIN SCROLL TURBOCHARGING

In a conventional turbocharger exhaust gas coming out of the cylinders is directed to a turbine, and the gas flow causes the turbine to spin. The turbine is mounted on a shaft that also spins, and at the other end of the shaft is a compressor wheel, which is fed air from the engine's air cleaner. The compressor wheel compresses the air, which is then sent to the engine's cylinders. Because the engine breathes in this high-pressure air rather than air at ambient pressure, a greater mass of air enters the cylinders. This means that each cylinder can burn more fuel – and that means it can produce more power.

Normally the exhaust gas from all the cylinders is collected together by the exhaust manifold and directed to the turbo. But because the exhaust gas from each cylinder is not a steady flow, but a series of pulses, there are pressure-wave effects in the manifold, which sometimes help and sometimes hinder the flow of gas to the turbo. A twin scroll or 'divided' turbo system splits the exhaust flow into two, pairing cylinders where the pulsating flows reinforce each other.

At the turbo there are two chambers, or scrolls, feeding gas to the turbine, each one fed by the exhaust from one pair of cylinders. One scroll feeds a nozzle at a steep angle to the inside of the turbine blades, which helps to accelerate the turbine from low speeds. This reduces turbo lag, the delay that happens when the driver suddenly demands more power and it takes a few moments for the turbine to speed up and boost pressure to rise. The other scroll feeds the outer part of the turbine blades, helping the turbo to spin faster and generate more boost.

The result is that a twin scroll turbo can provide improved response at low engine speeds yet still give good power at high revs. It's almost as though the engine has two turbochargers – a small one that responds quickly, and a big one that can deliver high boost. The downsides of the twin scroll turbo are the increased cost and complexity of the turbocharger itself and the exhaust manifold that feeds it, and the greater bulk of the whole assembly. In Jaguar Land Rover's case, space was not a problem as most of the engine bays receiving the Ingenium engines were designed to be big enough to fit much bulkier V6s and V8s, so there was plenty of room around the comparatively tiny in-line four to fit the bigger turbocharger.

The twin scroll turbocharger provides better low-speed response while still delivering high top-end power.
JAGUAR

Using variable valve lift and duration, the 300PS Ingenium engine avoided the need for a throttle, removing a restriction from the intake that compromised power and efficiency.
JAGUAR

All engines need a method to control the amount of power they produce. A diesel engine, which can operate at a wide range of air-to-fuel ratios, can be controlled by altering the amount of fuel injected – less fuel injected means less power. In a spark-ignition engine the air-to-fuel ratio has to be more tightly controlled for the engine to run reliably, so a different method of controlling the power must be used. The normal way to do this is to incorporate a throttle valve in the intake system to reduce the amount of air admitted to the cylinders, as a result reducing the amount of fuel that burns and the amount of power produced.

The problem with this is that the engine wastes a lot of the power it produces trying to suck air into the cylinders through an intake system which is deliberately restricted by the throttle, and that means fuel consumption is increased. The throttle also has an impact on top-end power, because even when it is fully open, the throttle plate still presents a small restriction to the intake air flow.

The new Ingenium engine did not have a throttle. Instead it used a system that could continuously vary the lift and duration of the intake valves. The system was licensed from the German company Shaeffler, and had its origins in Fiat's MultiAir design. Instead of the cams operating the valves directly, as in a normal engine, they operated compact

hydraulic pumps via finger followers rocking on low-friction roller bearings. The oil pressure generated in the pumps then opened and closed the valves.

The action of the pump could be controlled by the engine management system, varying the valve lift from zero – the valve staying closed – to a maximum of 11mm. In this way the intake valves could do the job of the conventional throttle, determining how much air was admitted to the cylinders. The pumping losses that a throttle causes were reduced, and there was no restriction in the intake to hurt the ultimate power output. Another benefit was better response to the accelerator, because there was always a substantial mass of air in the intake system ready to enter the cylinders.

The system could also influence the way air flowed into the cylinders in other useful ways. When the engine was starting up, the intake valves were opened later in the combustion cycle and valve lift was kept low, providing very precise control over the amount of air in the cylinder, which helped to improve cold-start performance. During gentle cruising at low engine speeds the engine went into what was called a 'composite' mode, where the intake valve opened later and closed earlier, generating greater turbulence of the intake air flow to enhance combustion efficiency. As more power was needed the intake valve was opened earlier to admit more air, and the closure of the exhaust valve was delayed to get the most energy out of each charge of air/fuel mixture. Under full load the system delivered maximum valve lift and increased the opening duration for both the intake and exhaust valves to maximize the engine's power output.

Other areas of the 300PS Ingenium were novel, too. The exhaust manifolds were integrated into the cylinder heads and had coolant passages, so the engine coolant was rapidly warmed by the exhaust gas heat. This helped to reduce warm-up time, aiding fuel economy and emissions performance. The turbocharger ran in ceramic ball bearings to reduce friction, particularly during a cold start – a first for a Jaguar Land Rover petrol engine.

INGENIUM F-TYPES

Rumour had it that JLR had planned to replace the supercharged V6 engine in the F-type with a 3.0-litre straight-six Ingenium. That engine was announced in February 2019 and replaced the V6 in the Range Rover Velar. It was available in 360PS and 400PS versions, featuring both a twin scroll turbocharger and an electric supercharger. But the plan to use the six in the F-type was scrapped when it was found that the long engine – an in-line six is inherently longer than a V6 or V8 – would not fit under the low bonnet of the F-type. Major re-engineering of the car's front end structure would have

been necessary, which, given the relatively small production numbers of the sports car, was never going to be viable. But the 4-cylinder Ingenium was another matter.

As well as powering the XE, XF and F-Pace, the most powerful Ingenium 4-cylinder was dropped into a new version of the F-type. It delivered performance which, if not quite up to the level of the V6 or V8 cars, was quick enough for most people. The great advantage of the turbo four lay in efficiency: Jaguar said the 4-cylinder F-type offered a fuel economy improvement of more than 16 per cent compared to the V6 car.

The lighter engine also contributed to a weight reduction of 52kg (115lb) compared to the V6-engined cars, making the 4-cylinder F-type the lightest yet. Inevitably most of the weight loss came from over the front axle, improving the F-type's weight distribution – Jaguar said the weight moved one percentage point towards the rear – and enhancing its agility compared to its more powerful stablemates.

To match the reduction in weight the front spring rates were reduced by 4 per cent and the rears by 3 per cent, while the valving of the monotube dampers was revised using knowledge gained from the chassis tuning of the F-type SVR. The electric power-assisted steering was recalibrated, and there was a new torque vectoring by braking system, which could brake the inner wheels while cornering to minimize understeer. At the launch of the 4-cylinder models Jaguar's ride and handling expert Mike Cross said:

A 6-cylinder Ingenium engine would not fit in the F-type, so a 4-cylinder turbo was offered.
JAGUAR

We wanted the power and efficiency of the new 4-cylinder engine to be matched by levels of responsiveness that would make the F-type driving experience even more engaging and rewarding. The result of the intensive development process is an even better balance, an even more connected feel, and enhanced ride comfort. Enthusiasts will want to drive this car: this is a true F-type, with its own unique character.

From the outside the 4-cylinder models were discernible by their single, central exhaust outlet (while the V6 and V8 models retained their double and quad exhaust systems respectively). The 4-cylinder car's exhaust system had been carefully tuned, and while it produced a very different sound to the V6 and V8 F-types, it was by no means uninteresting, with characterful pops and bangs on gearchanges. All versions had an active exhaust system that reduced back pressure – and generated more noise – at higher revs, and the R-Dynamic model had a switchable active exhaust, which made savouring the sound that much easier.

The R-Dynamic also had upgraded wheels and tyres – as standard the 4-cylinder car had new lightweight 18in wheels with 245/45R18 tyres at the front, and 275/40R18s at the rear, and the R-Dynamic stepped up to 19in wheels, though the tyres were no wider. There were 19in and 20in wheel designs available as options across the range.

ABOVE LEFT: **4-cylinder F-types had a single, central exhaust outlet.**
JAGUAR

ABOVE RIGHT: **New, lightweight alloy wheels were fitted to the 4-cylinder cars. This is an R-Dynamic model with optional 20in wheels.**
JAGUAR

Jaguar F-Type 4-Cylinder (2017)

Chassis and body

Type	Aluminium monocoque chassis/body; two-door two-seat convertible

Engine

Location	Front engine, longitudinal
Block material	Aluminium alloy
Head material	Aluminium alloy
Cylinders	In-line four
Cooling	Water
Lubrication	Wet sump
Bore × stroke	83.0 × 92.4mm
Capacity	1999cc
Main bearings	Five
Valves/operation	4 valves per cylinder, twin chain-driven overhead camshafts per cylinder bank
Compression ratio	9.5:1
Fuel system	200-bar fuel injection
Induction system	Twin scroll turbocharger
Maximum power	296bhp (300PS) at 5,500rpm
Maximum torque	295lb/ft (400Nm) at 1,500–4,500rpm
Transmission	Rear-wheel drive; Quickshift eight-speed automatic transmission

Suspension and steering

Front	Double wishbones, coil springs, telescopic dampers and anti-roll bar
Rear	Double wishbones, coil springs, telescopic dampers and anti-roll bar
Steering	Rack and pinion, electromechanical assistance
Brakes	Front: 355mm ventilated discs
	Rear: 325mm ventilated discs
	Servo assisted

Dimensions

Length	4,482mm (176.5in)
Width	1,923mm (75.7in)
Height	Convertible: 1,307mm (51.5in)
	Coupé: 1,310mm (51.6in)
Wheelbase	2,622mm (103.2in)
Unladen weight	Convertible: 1,545kg (3,406lb)
	Coupé: 1,525kg (3,362lb)

Performance

Top speed	155mph (250km/h)
Acceleration	0–60mph: 5.4sec

PRESS REACTION

Autocar's Matt Bird pitched the 4-cylinder F-type against its natural rival, Porsche's flat-four 718 Cayman. On twisty Welsh B-roads he found the four-pot F-type could keep up with the accomplished, mid-engined Porsche, despite its size. The 2-litre F-type had 'a resolve, precision and assuredness' that contrasted with the sometimes wayward nature of more powerful versions. The torque vectoring by braking system did a good job of keeping the F-type on the driver's chosen line.

Bird considered the combination of turbocharged Ingenium motor and eight-speed automatic transmission was 'interactive and engaging', and noted that the Jaguar was much shorter-geared than the Porsche. The Cayman had both a better ride and better body control, and marginally better steering, but the F-type's 4-cylinder soundtrack was more engaging. Bird concluded that the Cayman was the more satisfying sports car, but that the 4-cylinder F-type was Jaguar's strongest challenge to Porsche yet.

Road & Track said the 4-cylinder engine was a welcome change, which made the F-type more fun, with better steering and sharper handling. They were unable to match Jaguar's claimed 0–60mph time of 5.4sec, with a disappointing 6.7sec the best they could achieve – though the high temperature at their test track might have been the cause, as turbo engines always thrive on cool conditions. They praised the transmission, saying that the effectiveness of the sport mode made manual gearchanges unnecessary: 'The ghost of James Hunt possesses the automatic as it performs perfectly timed downshifts under braking, holds gears through corners, and clips off shifts at the 6,500rpm redline.' The 4-cylinder F-type worked, *Road & Track* said, because it looked just as good as the V6 and V8 models but cost a little less.

Evo's Antony Ingram looked under the F-type's bonnet and was surprised to see the engine mounted so far forward, and suggested that positioning it further back might have improved weight distribution and handling even further. Ingram said the car was still responsive but had a more consistent feel to its steering than the larger-engined F-types, with smoother turn-in. The engine was best in its lower and middle register, and the car was best left in Dynamic mode, which sharpened up response to the accelerator and encouraged the transmission to select shorter gears.

In *The Daily Telegraph* Andrew English reported that the 4-cylinder F-type drove 'beautifully' on the roads of North Wales, where JLR took many of their cars to hone their chassis balance. He praised the combination of the turbo engine and automatic gearbox, but noted that a 335bhp V6 manual F-type was only around £2,000 more and for that you got 'more torque and more fun'.

NAME CHANGES

In 2018 the F-type was upgraded to the latest 10in touch-screen infotainment system, and there was a new range of colours and wheel designs. On the technical side, torque vectoring by braking became standard across the range. There was also a new set of model names based on the power outputs in PS, which brought the F-type into line with other Jaguar Land Rover models. The 2.0-litre 4-cylinder F-type was now called the P300, the 335bhp V6 was called the P340, and what used to be the V6 S was now known as the P380. Both the P340 and P380 were available in standard or R-Dynamic trim levels. The V6-engined 400 Sport was dropped – Jaguar had said from the outset that it would only be available for a short period. At the top end of the range the V8 R and SVR models continued, and retained their existing names. In the UK, F-type prices now ranged from £50,910 for the P300 coupé, to £118,250 for the SVR convertible.

New for the SVR was a special graphics pack, which added body decals and special paint highlights. There was a contrast colour on the grille surround, mirror caps and the insides

The graphics pack for the SVR included decals, badges and a contrast-colour grille surround. This car is Corris Grey with Ultra Blue details.

JAGUAR

The nose decal included a '575' logo denoting the power output of the SVR. This car is Indus Silver.
JAGUAR

The '575' theme continued on the kickplates...
JAGUAR

...and on a badge between the seats.
JAGUAR

of the wing endplates, plus bonnet and sill decals with '575' graphics denoting the SVR's 575PS output. Inside the car the package added '575' sill protectors and a '575' badge between the seats. The package was available in five colour-ways: Yulong White/Firenze Red, Santorini Black/Gold, Corris Grey/Ultra Blue, Caldera Red/Black, Ultra Blue/Corris Grey and Indus Silver/Black.

CHEQUERED FLAG AND 2020MY

In October 2018 Jaguar announced a Chequered Flag special edition based on the F-type R-Dynamic Coupé and Convertible. The car was said to be 'in celebration of seventy years of Jaguar sports cars', referencing the 1948 introduction of the XK120 – and rather unfairly ignoring the pre-war SS Jaguar 100.

ABOVE: **The Chequered Flag special edition of 2018 celebrated seventy years of Jaguar sports cars.**
JAGUAR

The contrasting black roof echoed the optional carbon roof on the SVR.
JAGUAR

The Chequered Flag edition was available with either the 2.0-litre, 296bhp Ingenium turbo four or the 3.0-litre supercharged V6 in 335bhp or 375bhp form, all with the usual eight-speed ZF Quickshift automatic transmission. There was a choice of three colours – Caldera Red, Fuji White and Carpathian Grey – and the coupé had a contrasting black roof, visually similar to the optional carbon roof on the SVR but without the weight benefit. There was also an Exterior Black Design Pack, which included SVO extended side sills and 20in gloss-black, diamond-turned wheels that were exclusive to the car.

Inside the Chequered Flag edition there was black Windsor leather trim with contrast stitching, slimline Performance seats with chequered flag logos embossed into the headrests and optional heating and cooling, and a dark-

Performance seats had chequered flag logos on the headrests.

JAGUAR

Diamond-turned wheels were exclusive to the F-type Chequered Flag.

JAGUAR

The steering wheel also had a chequered flag logo, plus a red marker for the 'straight ahead' position.

JAGUAR

brushed aluminium centre console trim. The steering wheel had a red leather 'twelve o'clock' marker and a chequered flag logo on the middle spoke. For the first time in an F-type, the infotainment system incorporated Apple CarPlay and Android Auto to make it easier to connect to smartphones.

At the same time as the Chequered Flag was announced, Jaguar revealed enhancements across the F-type range for the 2020 model year (beginning in 2019). Damper settings were revised on the F-type R models, using lessons that had been learned from the SVR, improving ride comfort at low speed by reducing damping at wheel velocities below 0.3m per second by 24 per cent while stiffening the damping overall by 30 per cent. The F-type R also adopted the stiffer

rear knuckle and upper control arm from the SVR. All models now had a rear parking camera and front park aid as standard. The entry-level 4-cylinder car was now £51,925.

THE F-TYPE RALLY CAR

Shortly after the Chequered Flag edition was announced, Jaguar released details of two F-type convertible rally cars that took inspiration from the famous rally XK120 registered NUB120, which won three Gold Cups at the Alpine Rally in the early 1950s in the hands of Ian Appleyard. Though the rally cars were built to FIA specification they were not

F-type rally cars were inspired by the famous XK120, NUB120.

JAGUAR

intended to be competition cars – they were really just a bit of nostalgic fun.

The rally cars were powered by 2.0-litre Ingenium 4-cylinder engines driving through the usual eight-speed automatic gearbox. They were fitted with uprated brakes using grooved discs and four-piston calipers front and rear. There were new suspension springs that were softer than standard, and which provided 40mm (1.6in) more travel to cope with rough surfaces. Hand-built competition dampers came from EXE-TC in Devon, and featured remote oil reservoirs and three-way adjustability for fine control of the bump and rebound damping. Competition wheels were fitted with gravel rally tyres, and there was a limited-slip differential to improve power delivery on loose surfaces, plus a shorter final drive to improve acceleration.

The interior was simplified, and a hydraulic handbrake was added with a vertical lever to the left of the steering wheel to help drivers tackle hairpin bends. The centre exhaust box was removed, and underside protection plates fitted. The specification was completed with a full rollcage, racing bucket seats with six-point harnesses, a bonnet-mounted light pod and a fire extinguisher.

The rally cars were painted white, like NUB120, with a graphics package that was essentially a huge version of the Chequered Flag edition logo. The cars were tested at Walters Arena rally stage in South Wales, and were then put to work attending a variety of Jaguar events.

Driving one for *Autocar*, Dan Prosser pointed out that the rally F-type had too much weight and too little suspension travel to be a convincing competition rally car, but that it did achieve its aim of being fun to drive. Despite only having drive to the rear wheels, the F-type could accelerate rapidly on a loose surface provided the driver was sensitive with the throttle. But having fun seemed more to the point, as Prosser said: 'Much better to clog it and make the car slide.'

CAR's Adam Binnie noted that after start-up you had to click the steering wheel OK button a dozen times to clear a series of error messages relating to driver assistance systems that were no longer operational. He felt the handling of the rally car was progressive: 'The rear end of the F-type lets go inch by inch in a seemingly linear response to the openness of the throttle.' Binnie clearly enjoyed his time behind the wheel of the F-type rally car, concluding that it was likely to be one of the most thrilling cars he would drive all year.

The interior was simplified and fitted with competition seats and six-point harnesses.
JAGUAR

ABOVE: **The centre console gained a switch panel – note the big red fire-extinguisher button.**
JAGUAR

LEFT: **The hydraulic handbrake helped with hairpin bends.**
JAGUAR

BELOW LEFT: **A four-lamp pod was added to the bonnet.**
JAGUAR

OPPOSITE TOP: **Two 4-cylinder F-types were modified to rally specification.**
JAGUAR

OPPOSITE BOTTOM: **Junior Welsh Tarmac Rally Champion Jade Paveley gave the F-type rally car its final public demonstration at Wales Rally GB in 2019.**
JAGUAR

CHAPTER EIGHT

FUTURE OF THE F-TYPE

Prototypes of a facelifted F-type were seen testing in the summer of 2019 and Jaguar officially unveiled the revised car that December.

The styling was closely related to the old car's, but there were detail changes all around the car. The voluptuous shape of the new clamshell bonnet was said to have been inspired by the flowing curves of the C-type and D-type, and wider, shallower headlamps with J-shaped daytime running lights and a bigger egg-box grille gave the front end a new and more purposeful look. The slimmer LED lamps front and rear incorporated monogram patterns inspired by the lozenge-shaped Jaguar Heritage logo. But the modern shape

Design drawing for the facelifted F-type revealed in 2019, showing the reversed taper of the rear number plate recess.

JAGUAR

of the lamps distanced the car from the E-type – which had inspired elements of the 2012 F-type shape – and instead emphasized the new car's relationship with the rest of the contemporary Jaguar range, the rear lights referencing those of the I-Pace electric vehicle. Jaguar's 'leaper' mascot now appeared on the side vents. At the back, changing the shape of the registration plate recess so that it was wider at the bottom made the car look lower and wider.

Jaguar's exterior design director Adam Hatton said:

F-type has always had great proportions and stance, and our latest design is all about enhancing those key Jaguar values. Our aim was to make the car more contemporary, more purposeful, and even more dramatic.

Inside, the F-type gained a new 12.3in TFT instrument cluster with unique graphics offering a range of display modes, the default providing a large central rev counter. New interior details included subtle 'Jaguar Est. 1935' markings on the seat belt guides and glovebox release surround.

Under the skin the revised F-type followed a similar pattern, with no major changes but a package of detail improvements. The Ingenium four-cylinder engine, V6 and V8 were all carried over, though the V6 was no longer available in the UK, EU and some other world markets. Instead there was a new 450PS V8 offering 580Nm of torque from just 2,500rpm, while at the top of the range the F-type R now produced 575PS (566bhp), the same as the outgoing SVR. All the engines were mated to eight-speed Quickshift automatic transmissions, which were recalibrated using lessons learned on the Jaguar XE SV Project 8 to give swifter, more positive gearchanges. There was no longer any manual gearbox option.

Narrower lamps and a bigger grille made the front end bolder and more modern.
JAGUAR

LEFT: **Facelifted F-type clearly based on the 2012 car, but with more modern detailing.**
JAGUAR

BELOW: **The rear of the revised F-type looks lower and wider than before.**
JAGUAR

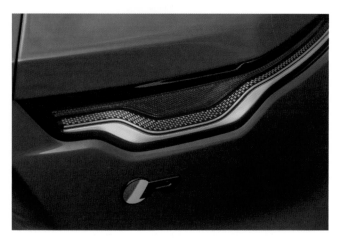

ABOVE: **The front and rear lamps of the revised F-type had monogram detailing inspired by the Jaguar Heritage logo.**

LEFT: **New side vents included the Jaguar 'leaper' mascot.**
JAGUAR

BELOW LEFT: **The revised interior included a 12.3in TFT instrument panel with a range of display modes.**
JAGUAR

ABOVE: *Glovebox release and seat belt guides paid subtle tribute to the birth of the Jaguar name more than eighty years ago.*

JLR'S FINANCIAL WOES

Since the F-type appeared in 2012 Jaguar Land Rover's story has been one of rising sales and increasing profits. The group sold 357,773 cars in 2012, rising year by year to a peak of 621,110 in 2017. Jaguar's sales more than tripled to over 180,000 cars over the same period, and the proportion of Jaguars in JLR's production rose from 16 per cent to 29 per cent. The increase in Jaguar sales was driven by the mid-range saloons and the advent of the F-Pace and E-Pace SUVs: being a specialist product the F-type was only a small part of the total, at around 5,000 cars a year.

But in February 2019 JLR posted its biggest ever quarterly loss of £3.4bn, and revealed that it anticipated it would lose money for the financial year as a whole for the first time in years. It put the losses down to a number of factors. Uncertainty over Britain leaving the EU, originally planned for March 2019, was one of them, causing some customers to delay plans to replace vehicles, and requiring the business to spend money planning for a variety of outcomes to ensure continuity of the supply chains for its manufacturing. Another factor was a backlash against diesel engines, which formed a large part of Jaguar's offer and was even more important for its stablemate Land Rover. Finally, Jaguar Land Rover was hit hard by a slowdown in the Chinese market, which resulted in fewer vehicle sales and a writedown in the value of its Chinese property and investments.

JLR's response was a programme of cost-cutting, including 4,500 redundancies across the business and the cancellation of some niche projects such as the Range Rover SV Coupé and Discovery SVX.

The F-type is never likely to generate enough sales to become a hugely profitable part of Jaguar's range, and as a result it will always be lower down the list of priorities than big-selling cars, which at the end of the 2010s means SUVs. But it is a useful 'halo' product – one that attracts attention and boosts the brand's image – so F-type fans will hope that JLR's management decides the investment needed to update it is justifiable.

FUTURE POWERTRAINS

Ford has been building engines for Jaguar at its Bridgend facility in South Wales since the 1990s. During Ford's ownership of the Jaguar brand it made sense for Jaguar to share Ford production facilities in Britain where extra capacity was needed – resulting in the Jaguar X-type being assembled at Ford's Halewood plant, and Jaguar engines being built alongside Ford units at Bridgend. Even after Jaguar was sold off in 2008 the engine supply deal between Ford and Jaguar was retained, and the Jaguar V6 and V8 engines in F-types are built in Wales (the 4-cylinder Ingenium engine is built at JLR's own engine plant near Wolverhampton).

The arrangement was due to continue until the end of 2020, but Jaguar announced in 2017 that it would be terminating the contract with Ford three months early, meaning that Bridgend production of Jaguar engines is now scheduled to end in September 2020. At that point three possible options exist for the future of the V6 and V8 engines.

It's possible that JLR could set up a new in-house production line for the AJ engines – this would most likely be at the Wolverhampton engine plant, alongside the Ingenium

production line. A second option is that JLR could outsource production of the engines to another company such as Cosworth (which has built a series of small-volume engines over the years) or Ricardo (which makes McLaren's M838T V8 engines). But neither of these scenarios seems likely, because the current Jaguar V8 is now ten years old, and its ancestry goes back to an engine designed in the mid-nineties. It's likely that the V8, and the V6 derived from it, are getting close to the end of their natural lives, and it would not make much sense to invest heavily in setting up a new manufacturing facility for engines that are not likely to be in production for very long.

Instead the most likely scenario is that the current V6 and V8 will drop out of Jaguar Land Rover's portfolio entirely at the end of 2020, and will be replaced by alternative engines. JLR's options are to develop new engines of its own, or to buy them from other manufacturers, and like its Gaydon neighbour Aston Martin, JLR appears to be taking both routes simultaneously – developing some of its own engines but buying in others.

The current V6 is being replaced across JLR's range by six-cylinder versions of the Ingenium engine. The Ingenium was designed from the outset as a modular engine family, with

The 6-cylinder Ingenium engine introduced in 2019 could feature in the F-type replacement.
JAGUAR

Jaguar Land Rover's Engine Manufacturing Facility near Wolverhampton: some of the next F-type's engines will be built here, though probably not all.
JAGUAR

the possibility of 3-, 4-, 5- and 6-cylinder versions. A 3.0-litre, 355bhp in-line six Ingenium engine has already been launched in Land Rover models to take the place of the V6. Rumour has it that the relatively tall and long in-line six will not fit in the current F-type, but it's likely that the next-generation car would be designed specifically to accommodate it.

As far as the V8s go at this stage there are only rumours about what will happen, but those rumours are that Jaguar Land Rover has done a deal with BMW for a 4.4-litre, twin-turbo V8 – codenamed Jennifer – to replace its own V8s in saloons, SUVs and sports cars. This may be a version of BMW's existing Munich-built N63 'hot VÉ' V8 engine,

BMW V8 engines are likely to power some future F-types.
BMW

recently seen in the new M850i coupé. A tuned variant, the S63, powers the new X5M and X6M models. But this family of engines is itself more than ten years old and must be nearing replacement, so it's not yet clear whether the Jennifer engine is a version of the N63, or based on the new motor that will take the N63's place in the next few years. Either way, the BMW-sourced V8 should produce at least 560bhp and be capable of 625bhp or more for performance models.

The current V8 could depart with a run-out model, which could use the 592bhp engine that has already been seen in the Jaguar XE Project 8. With 17bhp more than the V8 in the latest F-type SVR, this would improve the performance still further. And of course there is the potential for that engine to deliver even more power: tuning companies have already proved that 650bhp or more is within reach.

ELECTRIFIED F-TYPES

New engines are only half the story. JLR has already stated that from 2020 all its new vehicles will 'offer the option of electrification'. That could mean hybrid powertrains combining electric motors and petrol or diesel engines, or it could mean a fully electric powertrain such as the one in the I-Pace.

The C-X16 concept car that previewed the F-type in 2011 demonstrated a hybrid powertrain, and hybrid performance cars are now increasingly common – from BMW's i8 to hypercars such as the McLaren P1 and LaFerrari. A fully electric powertrain would be unusual, but not unprecedented for a sports car. Tesla's first product was the 2008 Roadster, based on the Lotus Elise, fitted with a single motor of up to 215kW output and a 450kg (992lb) battery pack holding up to 53kWh

Mercedes' SLS AMG Electric Drive shows that sports-car performance can be obtained from a pure-electric powertrain.
DAIMLER

of energy. The original Tesla Roadster could achieve 0–60mph in 3.7sec, a top speed of 125mph (201km/h), and in its final form had a range of up to 400 miles (640km). A new-generation roadster is now on the way, and Tesla claims 0–60mph in 1.9sec, a top speed of 250mph (402km/h), and a range of up to 620 miles (1,000km). The first version is set to cost £189,000, much more than an electric F-type is likely to be sold for.

Closer in size and specification to the F-type is the Mercedes-Benz SLS AMG Electric Drive, which was on sale from 2013 (at a cost of around £350,000). The SLS had four electric motors giving a total output of 552kW, powered by a 60kWh battery pack weighing 548kg (1,208lb). The SLS could reach 100km/h (62mph) from rest in 3.9sec, and go on to a top speed of 155mph (250km/h), with a potential range of 155 miles (250km).

Jaguar's I-Pace, introduced in 2018, shows how far electric drive technology has advanced in recent years. With two Jaguar-designed electric motors, one for each axle, the I-Pace has 395bhp at its disposal, with power coming from a much larger 90kWh battery pack. Range (using the much more stringent WLTP protocol) is up to 298 miles (480km), and the four-seater I-Pace can reach 60mph from rest in 4.5sec on the way to a maximum of 124mph (200km/h). It cost £58,995.

Jaguar's own I-Pace is one of the most accomplished electric vehicles, and points the way forward to electric Jaguars of the future.
JAGUAR

I-Pace's battery cells are mounted under the cabin floor, which gives the car a low centre of gravity – but such a design may not be possible for a sports car.
JAGUAR

MID-ENGINED F-TYPES

When General Motors replaced the C7-generation Chevrolet Corvette with the C8 in 2019 it broke with decades of tradition by switching from a conventional front engine/rear-drive car to a mid-engined format. Jaguar might choose to take the F-type in a similar direction in the long term.

One possibility that has been reported is that the front-engined F-type will be succeeded by a mid-engined hybrid, which would rival the Honda NSX, the Audi R8 and junior McLaren models. Because the model would be significantly different to the current car in its shape, engineering and ethos it would not carry over the F-type name, but might instead be called J-type (a name Jaguar applied to its trademark in the summer of 2018). *Auto Express* expected the car would have a V6 engine, but didn't say whether that would be Jaguar's own V6 or a motor from another source – an interesting question given the probable demise of the existing Jaguar V6 at the end of 2020. *Auto Express* said the hybrid car would have an electric motor on each axle to provide four-wheel drive.

There could also be a fully electric version to rival Porsche's new Taycan. The electric model could use two of the Jaguar-designed 150kW (200bhp) electric motors that were introduced on the I-Pace, probably with a larger 100kWh battery pack. Like the I-Pace, an electric F-type could include adjustable regenerative braking, allowing the driver to choose how much retardation was provided by the electric motor/generator units. But it's likely that battery and motor technology will have improved considerably between the launch of the I-Pace in 2018 and the time an electric F-type appears, which might mean that the amount of energy storage could be increased and more powerful motors could be fitted to give improvements in range and performance.

This four-wheel-drive, hybrid, mid-engined car would effectively be a revival of the C-X75 concept of 2010, which never made production – but did star in the 2015 James Bond film *Spectre*.

When could this radical new vision for the F-type become reality? To work that out we need to look at how long the current model might remain in production. The C-X16 concept that previewed the F-type made its public debut in 2011 and the production F-type convertible broke cover in 2012, so as this book goes to press the F-type is nearing its eighth birthday. The revisions introduced at the end of 2019 give the current car a few more years, but to get an idea just how much longer it is likely to remain in production we can look at the longevity of other recent Jaguar models.

X100, the first modern-generation XK, was in production for ten years. The second-generation XK, the X150, lasted nine years. Though the XKs were aimed at a slightly different market segment to the F-type, they are the closest parallels in Jaguar's recent past. Ian Callum has been quoted as saying that 'specialist cars' such as the F-type tend to have longer lives than mainstream models.

It's also worth looking at competitors: Porsche's 991-generation 911 bowed out in 2019 at the age of eight, while the previous 997 generation died at seven. The R231 Mercedes SL is likely to exit at eight or nine. The Aston Martin V8 Vantage survived to thirteen years before being

The mid-engined C8 Corvette might show the path that Jaguar will follow for future F-types.
GM

replaced by a new-generation car in 2018, and the DB9 managed twelve years before the DB11 replaced it in 2016. But by contrast the C7-generation Chevrolet Corvette was replaced after just six years in production.

Crunch all the numbers together and it suggests that the facelifted F-type could continue to around 2025. But for a manufacturer like Jaguar no model is created completely in isolation. Another key factor is the timing of the rest of Jaguar's model programme, and the workload that that imposes on the design and engineering teams. No car maker has the resources to work on every model all at once, so design and development has to be planned years in advance, taking into account likely sales performance, market trends and the conflicting needs of different models in the range. Most pressing for Jaguar right now is the renewal of the ageing XJ saloon, a replacement for which is expected in 2020. That is likely to be followed by replacements for the other Jaguar saloons and a new large SUV – possibly badged J-Pace – in the next few years.

HOW LONG CAN SPORTS CARS LAST?

By then petrol-engined sports cars could be living on borrowed time. In 2017 the French government announced plans to outlaw the sales of conventional petrol and diesel cars by 2040, and the British government followed suit. The British plans were to outlaw 'conventional' petrol and diesel vehicles, which might still open the door to sales of hybrids with internal combustion engines. Scotland set a target of 2032 for such a ban, and in 2018 a select committee of parliament urged the British government to adopt the same date. In response Mike Hawes of the Society of Motor Manufacturers and Traders, which represents the industry, said the existing 2040 target was 'challenging' and that a ban by 2032 was 'nigh-on impossible'. So current industry thinking is that there will still be cars on sale in the 2040s powered by internal combustion engines, though they may well be supported by electric motors in a hybrid powertrain.

Another issue facing the industry is the growth of driver assistance technology and ultimately a move to autonomous vehicles – cars that can drive themselves. Though autonomous technology has been demonstrated that can control a car in some circumstances, the problems of true autonomous capability are so substantial that it is likely to be decades before our cars will be able to drive themselves on all roads, at any time.

Jaguar explored some of the issues around fully autonomous cars in its 2017 Future-Type concept. This two-plus-one seater was envisaged as a car that could deliver itself to your door when it was needed and drive the more tedious parts of the journey for you, but would let you take over and drive yourself when you wanted. Jaguar's vision included an intelligent steering wheel it called Sayer, after the designer of the E-type, which would be the only part of the car you would actually own. Instead of buying a car, you would subscribe to a service that would provide whatever car you needed, summoned to you by your Sayer steering wheel.

The challenge for a brand such as Jaguar will be to embrace this new technology while at the same time retaining a unique character and appeal for its cars. But it will be many years yet before sports cars are a thing of the past – which means that F-types, in one form or another, should be with us for a long time to come.

CHAPTER NINE

F-TYPE OWNING AND DRIVING

Though the F-type sits in a narrow niche of the market, the number of different versions that have been available is surprisingly wide. Ignoring variations in trim and equipment there are three key choices to be made – about the body-style, the engine and the transmission.

Body style is simple enough: there are two mainstream choices, convertible and coupé, plus the rare Project 7 speedster. In the old days of British sports cars the choice would have been an easy one – the soft-top offers fun in the sun, but if you want to stay dry and warm when it's wet outside, take the coupé. Standards had moved on somewhat by the time the F-type came along and the convertible roof is much better-fitting than those of old. It is warmer, drier and quieter, too, thanks to a waterproof lining and a Thinsulate insulating layer. So the choice comes down to whether you prefer the open-top options provided by the convertible, or the rakish lines of the coupé, which, as with the E-type, has plenty of support as the better-looking of the two body styles.

There are three basic engine choices: a 2.0-litre in-line four, a 3.0-litre V6, and a 5.0-litre V8. All use forced induction, a turbo on the four and superchargers on the larger engines. There is only one specification of 4-cylinder engine in the F-type, with 295bhp, but the larger engines come in a range of power outputs. The V6 range starts with the 335bhp (340PS) unit, which was available from the launch in 2013. Alongside it was the 374bhp (390PS) V6 S, and in 2017–18 there was a 394bhp (400PS) 400 Sport V6. The V8s began with a 488bhp engine in the V8 S Convertible, followed by a 542bhp unit in the F-type R Coupé, and ultimately the 566bhp V8 of the Project 7 and SVR.

Generally the V6 cars are considered to be the best compromise between straight-line speed and handling. The 4-cylinder cars are still quick and they feel more agile to drive, while the V8s are arguably too powerful for their own good as everyday road cars. As second cars for fine days the V8s make more sense, and depreciation is such that earlier V8s are now selling secondhand for similar prices to new 4-cylinder F-types – making the choice rather more difficult. The best advice is to try the cars before you buy to get a feel for the different models.

Coupé style and practicality or convertible fun and glamour? One of several choices a potential F-type buyer needs to make.
JAGUAR

The vast majority of these cars are eight-speed automatics, though some models were also available with six-speed manual gearboxes. F-types are available with two- and four-wheel drive, the latter only with V6 and V8 engines and always with automatic transmission. For some people the manual gearbox adds a vital extra layer of driver engagement, but for most people the ZF automatic transmissions with their manual shift paddles do a perfectly good job.

LEFT: **The V8-engined F-type R is considered by many to be too lairy for everyday use, but it makes a fun weekend car.**
AUTHOR

F-TYPE MODELS OVERVIEW

Model	Years	Transmission	Power	0–60	Max	Economy
2.0 I4 turbo conv/coupé	2017–	8sp auto	295bhp	5.4sec	155mph	35mpg
2.0 I4 turbo R-Dynamic conv/coupé	2017–	8sp auto	295bhp	5.4sec	155mph	35mpg
3.0 V6 conv/coupé	2013–17	8sp auto	335bhp	5.1sec	161mph	33mpg
3.0 V6 conv/coupé	2017–	8sp auto	335bhp	5.1sec	161mph	28mpg
3.0 V6 R-Dynamic conv/coupé	2017–	8sp auto	335bhp	5.1sec	161mph	28mpg
3.0 V6 conv/coupé	2015–17	6sp man	335bhp	5.5sec	161mph	28mpg
3.0 V6 conv/coupé	2017–	6sp man	335bhp	5.5sec	161mph	27mpg
3.0 V6 R-Dynamic conv/coupé	2017–	6sp man	335bhp	5.5sec	161mph	27mpg
3.0 V6 S conv/coupé	2015–17	6sp man	374bhp	5.3sec	171mph	28mpg
3.0 V6 S conv/coupé	2013–17	8sp auto	374bhp	4.8sec	171mph	32mpg
3.0 V6 S AWD conv/coupé	2015–17	8sp auto	374bhp	4.9sec	171mph	31mpg
3.0 V6 S AWD British Design conv/coupé	2016–17	8sp auto	374bhp	4.9sec	171mph	31mpg
3.0 V6 R-Dynamic conv/coupé	2017–	6sp man	374bhp	5.3sec	171mph	26mpg
3.0 V6 R-Dynamic conv/coupé	2017–	8sp auto	374bhp	4.8sec	171mph	28mpg
3.0 V6 AWD R-Dynamic coupé	2017–	8sp auto	374bhp	4.9sec	171mph	27mpg
3.0 V6 400 Sport conv/coupé	2017–18	8sp auto	394bhp	4.8sec	171mph	32mpg
3.0 V6 AWD 400 Sport conv/coupé	2017–18	8sp auto	394bhp	4.9sec	171mph	31mpg
5.0 V8 S conv	2013–15	8sp auto	488bhp	4.2sec	186mph	25mpg
5.0 V8 AWD R conv/coupé	2017–	8sp auto	542bhp	3.9sec	186mph	25mpg
Project 7	2015	8sp auto	566bhp	3.8sec	186mph	n/a
5.0 V8 AWD SVR conv/coupé	2016–17	8sp auto	566bhp	3.5sec	200mph	25mpg
5.0 V8 AWD SVR conv	2017–	8sp auto	566bhp	3.5sec	195mph	25mpg
5.0 V8 AWD SVR coupé	2017–	8sp auto	566bhp	3.5sec	200mph	25mpg

Years are calendar years – model years will run one or two years ahead. Coupé models introduced 2014. Economy is the official combined mpg figure.

SAFETY RECALLS

F-types have been subject to a number of recalls for safety-related concerns. Generally these are precautionary, attending to issues that have been identified on a small number of vehicles just in case there is a wider problem. Recalls are common across the industry and nothing to worry about, as long as the appropriate action has been taken in response. Usually this involves contacting a Jaguar dealer and taking the vehicle in for rectification work, which should be free of any charges for parts or labour.

On F-types built between 10 and 25 June 2014 there is a risk of high-speed instability due to a failure of the pop-up rear spoiler to deploy. The engine management system

---

F-TYPE CLUBS AND FORUMS

The F-type is well served by specialist communities, ranging from online owners' forums to Jaguar clubs either dedicated to the F-type or with an F-type section. The clubs charge for membership but offer extra benefits such as discounts, magazines and events, while the forums tend to be less comprehensive in the benefits they offer but are usually free to join.

Jaguar Enthusiasts' Club

The largest Jaguar Club in the world. Monthly *Jaguar Enthusiast* magazine, plenty of events, and an online forum with an F-type section. UK membership: £45 (+£5 in the first year).

Jaguar Enthusiasts' Club
Abbeywood Office Park
Emma Chris Way
Filton
Bristol
BS34 7JU
Tel: +44 (0) 1179 698186
Fax: +44 (0) 1179 791863
Email: office@jec.org.uk
Website: jec.org.uk

Jaguar Drivers' Club

The original Jaguar club, formed in 1956. *Jaguar Driver* magazine, discounts, events, technical advice and more. UK membership: from £36.

Jaguar House
18 Stuart Street
Luton
Bedfordshire
LU1 2SL
Tel: +44 (0) 1582 419332
Fax: +44 (0) 1582 455412
Email: enquiries@jdclub.co.uk
Website: www.jaguardriver.co.uk

F-type Enthusiasts Club

Founded in May 2014 and dedicated solely to the F-type. Digital magazine and newsletters, members-only forum, events, discounts and more. UK or overseas membership: £40.

Unit 2 (Basepoint)
The Old Rectory
Springhead Road
Northfleet
Kent
DA11 8HN
Tel: +44(0)1474 886946
Email: mark.gregory@f-typeec.co.uk
Website: www.f-typeec.co.uk

F-type Forums

Internet forum for F-type enthusiasts. Lively conversations with owners all over the world. UK membership: free.

Email: info@ftypeforums.co.uk
Website: www.ftypeforums.co.uk

Jaguar Forums F-type forum

US-based internet forum for F-type enthusiasts. Lots of posts from the USA but also from other owners around the world. UK membership: free.

Website: www.jaguarforums.com/forum/f-type-x152-72/

should restrict the speed of the car to 137mph (220km/h) in these circumstances, but this may not occur. These vehicles need to have new software installed.

V6-engined F-types built between 18 August and 2 October 2014 were deemed at risk of fire due to a loose positive cable fixing at the alternator. There were also concerns about the fixings for belt-driven engine ancillaries such as the power-steering pump, failure of which could result in sudden loss of steering assistance, potentially causing a crash. The vehicles should be recalled for inspection and tightening of the fixings to the correct specification.

V6 convertible F-types with all-wheel drive and constantly variable damping built between 10 September 2014 and 14 March 2015 were fitted with incorrect rear anti-roll bars. If the vehicle begins to oversteer, the stability control (DSC) system will be unable to prevent a loss of control. These vehicles need the rear anti-roll bar removed and replaced with the correct specification item.

F-types with electric power-assisted steering built between 9 and 24 February 2015 may have been released with the steering set to an incorrect mode. As a result a failure in the system could cause it to create unexpected steering inputs that the driver might be unable to control, with an obvious risk of a crash. On these vehicles new software must be uploaded or, in certain cases, the steering rack replaced with one to the correct specification.

F-type SVR models from the 2017 model year built between 12 January and 15 August 2016 may have had a bolt retaining the rear lower suspension control arm to a rear knuckle joint incorrectly tightened. Failure could affect stability of the vehicle. These vehicles should have the bolt replaced and correctly tightened.

On F-types built between 16 February 2016 and 16 December 2016 the seat-belt pre-tensioners may fail to deploy, and on these vehicles the seat-belt tensioners should be checked and if necessary replaced.

F-type 2.0-litre models built before 17 August 2017 are at risk of fuel leaks caused by inconsistent brazing of the fuel rail end caps. This can cause fuel to leak into the engine bay, which may cause a fire. On these vehicles the fuel rail must be replaced with a correctly manufactured version.

On 2018 model year F-types built between 16 December 2016 and 24 April 2017 there is a risk that one or both front indicators may fail with no warning to the driver. This can be resolved by updating the vehicle with new software.

Another recall, which appears to affect only North American market F-types built between 31 August 2012 and 22 October 2014, concerns the wiring for control modules relating to the airbag system. These vehicles should have the system wiring reconfigured.

WHAT TO LOOK FOR

Independent Jaguar Land Rover specialist Tom Lenthall (0118 973 1614, www.tomlenthall.co.uk) has considerable experience working with F-types, and has identified a number of weak spots to bear in mind when looking at cars to buy.

The aluminium body of the F-type cannot rust, but still has problems to be aware of. Repair of accident damage can be more difficult and time-consuming than with steel panels, so cars with parking knocks or more serious damage are likely to need considerable expenditure to get them back to perfect condition.

A common issue is that the steel braces under the car quickly begin to rust. This is often only surface rust and no more than a cosmetic issue, but in some cases the damage has been severe enough to require replacement. On high-mileage cars check for stone chips at the front of the rear arch where it swells outwards, and on the sills, as the paint protection film used does not cover a very large area. The pop-out door handles have been known to fail, so check they work correctly on both doors. Some owners report the bonnet bending out of shape if closed by pressing down on one side – it needs to be closed with a firm push near the centre of the rear edge.

F-types have a pedestrian safety system that pops the bonnet up by 130mm (5.1in) if it detects an impact, so that a pedestrian landing on the bonnet is well cushioned. Some owners have experienced the system going off unexpectedly, for example when the nose is grounded on a speed ramp, leading to a significant repair bill. The system is armed at between 12mph and 31mph (19km/h and 50km/h), so many owners ensure they tackle speed ramps at 10mph (16km/h) or less to avoid the problem.

Electrical faults are one of the most common bugbears with the F-type. As with many modern vehicles a healthy battery is essential to avoid spurious warning lights and messages. On convertibles the roof motors can give problems, so when buying it's important to check that the roof lowers and raises without noises or juddering. As with any fairly modern car the F-type has dozens of sensors and actuators and in time they can give problems.

Underbody braces can corrode. This one has been stripped and repainted by Jaguar specialists Tom Lenthall.
TOM LENTHALL LTD

Sills and rear arches can suffer from stone chips to the paint.
AUTHOR

An emerging issue is of corrosion affecting a power-supply box in the wheel arch on the driver's side (on right-hand-drive cars). To make a proper repair the connector block has to be taken off so the corrosion can be removed and the area painted for protection, after which a new mounting bolt can be fitted. The connector block is then refitted, grease applied to keep water out of the electri-cal connections, and the connector cover fitted and water sealed.

Inside the car the inflatable bolsters on some seats can fail, so check for correct operation. Some taller drivers find the Performance seats uncomfortable after a while, so try to spend a reasonable amount of time in the car to make sure the seat fits you. Listen out for trim squeaks and

ABOVE LEFT: **Pop-out door handles have been known to fail, so check they work correctly on both doors.**
AUTHOR

ABOVE RIGHT: **Sound systems can generate trim rattles.**
JAGUAR

rattles, which can develop on high-mileage cars. The upgrade Meridian stereo system can also excite trim vibrations, so play some loud and bassy music to check. Another common issue is that the rising centre air vent can fail.

Scratches to side windows are quite common due to grit collecting in the window seals, so examine the windows carefully.

The 300PS Ingenium petrol engine is too new for any pattern of problems to have become established yet, but the V6s and V8s have been around a long time and are a well-known quantity. Generally they are reliable units, though there have been problems with failing injectors – if one stops working it seems common for others on the same engine to fail before long. Noisy tappets, worn cam-chain tensioners, wheezing superchargers and failing fuel pumps are also reported. A common issue is that the active valves in the exhaust system stop being active and stick in the open position, leading to an excessively noisy exhaust. The fix is a new rear exhaust box.

The ZF automatic transmissions are largely fault free, but some specialists suggest changing the fluid at 70,000 miles (113,000km) despite the official line of the box being filled for life. Differentials tend to have problems with leaks from the main oil seal. The suspension can suffer from split rubber bushes and deteriorating tie-bar dust covers, both of which can result in an MOT failure.

The electrical connection block behind the front wheel can start to corrode.
TOM LENTHALL LTD

ABOVE LEFT: **Active exhaust valves can seize open leading to a permanently loud exhaust.**
AUTHOR

ABOVE RIGHT: **Carbon ceramic brakes are only essential for very hard use, but do offer virtually dust-free and maintenance-free operation.**
AUTHOR

The steel disc brake systems show little signs of fade unless driven seriously hard, so the carbon ceramic upgrade is an expensive luxury unless you intend to drive your F-type close to its limits on a regular basis. However, the carbon ceramic system does have two advantages to be aware of: unlike a conventional brake system it generates virtually no brake dust to sully the surface of the wheels, and the pads and discs will last the lifetime of the car.

While this list of problems that the F-type can suffer from might look daunting, in practice owners often experience only occasional niggles or no problems at all. And there are plenty of enthusiastic F-type owners to demonstrate that running one of these cars can be a real pleasure.

JAGUAR PROJECT CODES
1975–2019

Jaguar development projects used XJ – for 'eXperimental Jaguar' followed by a number since the 1960s (XJ1 was Jaguar's first V12 engine project). The numbers were roughly chronological, though there were many anomalies. Under Ford ownership in the 1990s projects were given codes with an X followed by three digits, which mirrors Land Rover's L codes. In recent years Jaguar's public concept cars have had C-X codes, but the real behind-the-scenes development still goes on under X numbers. The codes are arranged in vehicle families: the F-type and other sports car/GT projects have 'X1..' codenames.

Vehicles

ALC	Advanced Lightweight Coupé – XK preview (2005)
C-XF	XF saloon preview (2007)
C-X16	Hybrid sports car – F-type preview (2011)
C-X17	SUV – F-Pace preview (2013)
C-X75	Hybrid supercar (2010)
XJ4	XJ saloon (1968)
XJ25	E-type Series 3 V12 2+2 (1971–74)
XJ26	E-type Series 3 V12 roadster (1971–74)
XJ27	XJ-S (1975–96)
XJ28	XJ-S convertible – cancelled
XJ40	XJ saloon (1986)
XJ41	F-type coupé related to XJ40 – cancelled
XJ42	F-type convertible version of XJ41 – cancelled
XJ50	XJ Series III V12 (1979–92)
XJ57	XJ-S AJ6 coupé (1983–96)
XJ58	XJ-SC AJ6 cabriolet (1983–88)
XJ63	XJ-S AJ6 coupé with Getrag manual gearbox
XJ71	XJ-S development car for XJ41
XJ77	XJ-S V12 convertible
XJ78	XJ-S AJ6 convertible

XJ79	XJ-S four-wheel-drive development car
XJ81	XJ40-based V12 saloon (1992)
XJ87	XJ-S V12 coupé facelift (1991–6)
XJ88	XJ-S AJ6 coupé facelift (1991–6)
XJ89	XJ-S cabriolet facelift
XJ97	XJ-S V12 convertible facelift (1991–6)
XJ98	XJ-S AJ6 convertible facelift (1991–6)
XX	TWR-led successor to XJ41/42 – developed into Aston Martin DB7
X100	XK8/XKR coupé/convertible (1996)
X150	XK/XKR coupé/convertible (2006)
X152	F-type coupé/convertible (2013)
X200	S-type saloon (1998)
X202-4	S-type revisions – last digit denotes model year
X250	XF saloon (2008)
X260	XF saloon (2016)
X300	XJ saloon (1994)
X305	XJ V12 saloon (1994)
X308	XJ saloon (1997–2002)
X350	XJ saloon with alloy structure (2002–9)
X351	XJ saloon (2009–)
X358	XJ saloon – X350 facelift (2007)
X400	X-type saloon (2001)
X590	I-Pace electric vehicle (2018)
X600	F-type concept (2000)/Mid-engined F-type – cancelled
X760	XE saloon (2015)
X761	F-Pace SUV (2015)

Engines

AJ6	2919/3239/3590/3980cc I6, all alloy replacement for XK twin-cam, (1983–94)

AJ16	3239/3980cc I6 developed from AJ6 for XJS and XJ6 (1994–97)
AJ-V6	Jaguar version of Ford Duratec V6, 2.1/2.5/3.0 (2000–2011)
AJ-V8	V8 for XK8/XJ (1996–)
AJ20	2099cc AJ-V6 for X-type
AJ25	2495cc AJ-V6 for X-type and S-type
AJ26	3996cc AJ-V8 for XK8, XJ8; also supercharged AJ26S for XKR, XJR (1996–98)
AJ27	Update of AJ26 with variable valve timing; also supercharged AJ27S for XKR, XJR (1999–2003)
AJ28	Update of AJ27 for S-type (2000–2)
AJ30	2967cc AJ-V6 for X-type, S-type, XF
AJ33	4196cc AJ-V8 for XK; also supercharged AJ33S for XKR, XJR, S-type R, XF (2003–6)
AJ34	Updated AJ33 with variable valve timing for XK, S-type, XJ8, XF; also supercharged AJ34S for XKR, XJR, S-type R, XF (2006–2010)
AJ35	3934cc AJ-V8 built by Ford in USA
AJ37	4280cc AJ-V8 built in Germany by Aston Martin for the V8 Vantage (2005–15)
AJ41	4394cc AJ-V8 for Land Rover

AJ-V8 Gen III	Revised AJ-V8 with new cylinder block (2009–)
AJ126	2995cc V6 based on AJ-V8 Gen III for F-type, XE, XF, F-Pace and Land Rover (2014–)
AJ133	AJ-V8 Gen III for F-type, XF, XJ, XK, XFR, XJR, XKR and Land Rover (2009–)
AJ200	Ingenium 1999cc in-line four for F-type, XE, XF, XJ, F-Pace, E-Pace and Land Rover (2015–)
Jennifer	BMW-sourced 4.4-litre V8 for future models

Platforms

CDW27	Ford Mondeo platform: X-type
DEW98	Ford Thunderbird/Lincoln LS platform: S-type, XF
D2a	X351 XJ
D6a	F-type
D7a	iQ-Al platform – F-Pace, XE, 2021 XJ
D7e	iQ-Al platform – I-Pace
D7u	iQ-Al platform – used by Land Rover
D8	LR-MS platform developed from Ford EUCD – E-Pace

INDEX